From Tongues of Temple Bells

(The Best of Oriental Philosophy)

From Tongues of
Temple Bells
(The Best of Oriental Philosophy)

by William R. Sickles

South Brunswick and New York: A. S. Barnes and Company
London: Thomas Yoseloff Ltd

Library of Congress Catalogue Card Number: 73-88293

A. S. Barnes and Co., Inc.
Cranbury, New Jersey 08512

Thomas Yoseloff Ltd
108 New Bond Street
London W1Y OQX, England

SBN 498 07426 9

Printed in the United States of America

DEDICATED to the memory of:

DR. REES EDGAR TULLOSS, late president
of Wittenberg University,
DR. GEORGE W. HARTMANN, late professor
at Columbia University, and
DR. EGON BRUNSWIK, late professor at the
University of California, Berkeley.

All were teachers, but more importantly, were
rare personalities who enriched the world about
them. And all were true friends in the old fashioned meaning of that term. Few have been so
fortunate as I.

Contents

Contents

Preface

Not too long ago, *Life* magazine carried an article entitled "Year of the Guru"—a Sanskrit term for "teacher." The purpose was to call attention to the recent and surprisingly active interest in oriental philosophy that is sweeping America. Such interest has continuously existed at low ebb, of course, and in the past one could always find those who were knowledgable in the Vedanta. However, now and then it seems that certain events bring about a high tide of public interest in this mode of thought. Prior to the unparalleled upsurge now going on, for example, periods of intensified popular involvement can be associated with such events as (1) the founding of the American Vedanta Society by Swami (Master) Vivekananda, ca. 1890, (2) the publications of Rabindranath Tagore in the early 1900's, and (3) the relatively recent and broadly circulated works of Khalil Gibran. It is perhaps significant that these latter (similar in some respects to the present writings) went through numerous printings and influenced literally millions of readers.

What accounts for the sudden popularity of oriental precepts amidst the violence of today's America? Only the perspective of history will enable one to answer this with any degree of certainty. However, one fact has already become obvious. The movement is spreading at a rate far exceeding that of any previous revival. What was once commonly assumed to be the province of the elderly and scholarly is now being adopted by ever-increasing

9

proportions of the younger set. As a result, side-effects are even spilling over into such peripheral media as clothing fashions and taste in music.

The above observations may be considered prologue to the work offered here. In actuality, these writings are the culmination of about forty years of sporadic study in the area. They first found expression in a series of ten weekly half-hour radio broadcasts presented "in the public interest" over Station KCSU in Utah. Each was accompanied (at opening and close) by music native to the culture treated in that particular broadcast.

This was twenty years ago, and though subsequently expanded and edited, the plan of the present book follows in the main that of the original broadcast series. Each "chapter" is set in a different culture. A story is taken from that culture—sometimes fictional, sometimes historical—and this is then turned into a vehicle, as it were, to carry the philosophy. Descriptions, references to places and things, figures of speech, and other verbal trappings, are authentic and accurate. For the curious and scholarly, the less obvious of these are explained in notes at the end.

For these reasons, the work is admittedly different from the usual compendia of oriental philosophy. For one thing, it is believed to be more readable. It is not filled with dry quotations. Rather, the intent is to present certain philosophical themes that have played through the thinking of bygone cultures, and to do this in a semi-narrative fashion by embedding such thinking in the contexts of stories taken from those cultures. As an aging guru, I only hope they are as interesting to read as they were to write and deliver.

From Tongues of Temple Bells

(The Best of Oriental Philosophy)

1
City of the Horizon

Egypt! More than three thousand and two hundred years have rolled their sands back from the Empress of the Nile.

Behold—on every side these shifting sands which caress the stone faces of the Ancients, whispering to them with the voices of centuries.

And among these whispers there was singing, and the song was a hymn to Aton[1]—the living Aton—and the sands spoke, saying:

"Call upon my name unto eternity, and it shall not fail."[2]

And I called, and lo! Akhnaton, Pharaoh of Egypt,[3] arose from the cliffs of the evening light, arose and opened before my eyes the City of the Horizon!

The bones of the earth-gods trembled. The metal of the sky burst asunder. And the columns of the city stood erect, embraced in the arms of the morning sun.

Standing light and slender as a maiden mirrored in the emerald waters of the Nile, was Akhetaton—City of the Horizon![4]

To the north, the royal palace raised itself against the sky—five hundred two and forty pillars, the tops of which were carved as palm leaves. And on each leaf there were rich stones clutched in petals of gold, and the onyx and the moonstone reflected colored lights against the walls.

Beneath the pillars of the palace, pavements of tinted glass caught the rays of the sun and came to life with

13

pictures of red poppies, wild geese rising in flight from the marshes, butterflies, buds of the papyrus, and figures of leaping antelopes.

To the south, Maru-Aton, "Precinct of the Sun,"[5] stood beside an artificial lake. A thin bridge led from the portico temple, between two kiosks with pillared fronts, to a small island edged with blossoms of the water-lotos. And in the lake, the imaged pillars of the island temples waved like long white ribbons on the water.

So it was when the sun (whose footsteps are the day) was sung to sleep by the soft voice of Nefertiti,[6] the plucking of lutes, and the music of the systrums and the timbrels. And darkness wrapped her gown about the City of the Horizon.

On the pavilion by the lake, bright with festoons of flowers hung from the mouths of brazen cobras, beautiful maidens danced without dress to the flowing of the music —music of ancient Egypt, lovelier than the hymns of Adonis, or the chants of Baal.

And upon the lake, pleasure boats, decked with colored ostrich plumes from Lybia, glided among the water flowers —and over all lay the faint light from candles within thin vases of alabaster which stood on pillars in the water.

More beautiful than the terraced myrrh-gardens of Hatshepsut,[7] was Maru-Aton! Strange incense trees from Punt dipped their leaves into her waters, and the odors of fragrant gums from Araby mixed with the scent of roses in the summer winds.

Tame panthers, black as the Kingdom of Osirius, and leashed by Negro slaves, slept upon the steps, and the lights from the vases played upon their collars of amber and gold—gold from the mines of the eastern desert, amber from Punt.

Upon the pavilion, the lights glinted on the armor of Mai, General of the Armies, who gossiped with the girls and drank wines fetched by Nubian slaves from the cellars beneath the colonnades that fringed the northern shore. And in the shadows, Bek, chief of the sculptors, sat on the faience tiles and ate from a basket of pomegranates, grapes, and melons.

And on still another pavilion, beneath an arcade which spanned the water garden, sat the Pharaoh, Akhnaton, and in his heart was grief—the death-dance of the Muu.

About his neck hung the golden Ankh, symbol of life[8]— the rhythm of the heat that is the sun—but he foresaw the ending, and the evening of the gods, and the fall of the City of the Horizon, when not one stone would be left standing on another.[9]

Thus, darkly ran the thoughts of Akhnaton, as a vision and an omen of that day when the moralizers and the priesthood of Amen would destroy his city and erase his name from the scroll of the honored.

And on the next day, when the rites of the sunrise were done, he summoned his vizier, Nakht, and the high-priest, Meryra, and all the nobles who lived in the City of the Horizon, and he spoke to them as follows:

In the moonlight of the last watch, while the sun was behind the western hills, I lived with the Ancients, examined their writings, and studied their words, and I now make this declaration to you:

Throughout the past, I built for the future. Now, the future does not exist. And when I look upon the ruins of my past, I see my temple standing perfect—it is the present!

And lo! Before me opens a new world, and a different world—the world of that-which-is. What to me, now, is the man of tomorrow? Less, less than myself to the man before!

The past is only the past to the present. It is not the past to the past. Only the present has being. How my heart hurts that I have so often thrown it away!

The child dreams of tomorrow. The aged one dreams of yesterday. But when the future and the past are laid one upon the other, there is only the present—which is the dream.

And such is the present that, between our yesterday and our tomorrow, lives the changing day—for change is the only unchanging thing.

He who lives within the day, therefore, becomes a part of change itself, and thereby makes himself unchanging. He has reached the present—and also immortality.

Footsteps leading into the present, the Here and Now, are steps leading into life. This is all that can exist. This is life.

Say to yourself: 'This day is my own, and I am happy herein—for it encompasses all eternity, which is mine.'

Yesterday was today. Today will be tomorrow. And in the *is* is all the *was* and all the *will be*.

There is a Here in every There, and a Now in every Then. And he who does not find it so, loses much of life.

The present should not be lived in terms of the future. Was the past lived in terms of the present? Can there be two days in one?

Study the child—for he has no past. He lives in the present only. For this reason he is trusting, honest, sincere, and happy. If you would be happy, as he is, then live as he lives—in the present.

Every day, as one grows older, he becomes less capable of living fully. He who lives for the future, therefore, never really succeeds in living; and he never regrets what he has done half so much as what he has not done.

When one has renounced that which might have added happiness to his life, when he has denied the heart—to that degree has he died!

The joys of the day are not so many as its hours, and when the day is gone, only the joys are remembered. Therefore, he lives doubly long and well who lives joyously. But he who lives in grief does not live long—even in his own memory.

Life is the aim of life. Man is a goal and an ideal in himself. Oh, my friends, follow your heart in the Here and Now![10]

Woe! Woe unto him whose understanding deserts the heart, who tears the mind from out the body, who no longer casts a shadow in the living sun of the Now!

Advise with your heart in all things. Though sometimes mistaken, it is never disloyal. And a man may profit from his mistakes—but a man's disloyalty to himself makes all things impossible.

So I say it—let not your inner-man be the servant of your outer-man, or you will be filled with ghosts!

No thought can live without the heart, and no thought can die until the heart has canceled it.

Habit, love, curiosity—these are a part of the reasons men act, and not reason itself. They follow their hearts, not their heads.

Reason is not the guide of life. It is merely one of the handmaidens of the heart.

Let this be your guide—that you should so dwell within the hours that the pleasures of tomorrow may be heightened by the memories of today.

He who has the present has everything. Tell me what

I can do after fifty years—I shall do it now!

He does everything who does it today—and nothing if he leaves it for tomorrow.

However, no amount of knowledge of the Here and Now can lead you to conclude what *will be,* or what *ought to be.*

The duty that is no longer a pleasure ceases to exist as such.

There is only one all-important duty—that of being happy. Remember, whatever happens, it is your greatest obligation to yourself to derive advantage and happiness from it.

The greatest skill of living is to learn how to turn into pleasure a goodly part of that which might have been pain.

Live today. Be natural. Know that nature is not sad—for only man is sad, and strangely enough, only man is blessed with laughter.

Laugh at the absurdities of the solemn. Your future lies in laughter. It holds your friends. It bewilders your enemies.

Stare not at your feet. You were born to stand erect, to follow your heart—to throw back your head and laugh!

Man is the most recent animal, and joy is the heritage of his youth. Oh, how I wish his life and his today absorbed him half as much as his death and his tomorrow!

Death is the whispered promise: clip not the wings of hours—and they will return bearing with them tomorrow, and the fruits of tomorrow. But these are lie-cankers in the heart, and a denial of today—for there never was tomorrow, nor shall there ever be.

The dead of today are yesterday's men who lived for tomorrow!

Every day has been tomorrow to a day that now is past. And he who seeks the fields of tomorrow must cross the marshes of yesterday. But keep this in mind—that he who enters the past remains in the past. One cannot catch up with time itself.

Happiness, O my friends, is in the light of today's sun. It burns away the cares of yesterday.

But when one turns his back to the sun, even the shadow of his own image becomes distorted on the earth.

Face the sun! Let the shadows fall behind you!

If one is anxious about the future, or sorrowful about the past, it is merely because he does not recognize the present.

Happiness is in the light of today's sun, and happiness is the highest good in life—for every value is based on *what* we like, and *how much* we like it.

They that abstain from pleasures are not the masters of pleasure, but slaves that tremble in fear of their own hearts!

Only the strong of heart are the masters of pleasure— and of all other things!

Stand not in fear of your heart, but follow it, no matter where it leads. For those whose minds are servants to their hearts, there shall be no yesterdays.

But for those who fear the heart, each morning sun shall carry shadows from the blackness of before. And the hour will come, in this gathering of the shadows, when the sun cannot be seen. And solemnity and old age will silence laughter in the fearfulness of night—when there is no light for sporting in the fields, nor new temptations.

O my friends! Dwell in the desire of your hearts—for when nothing is desired, all things are feared.

To desire the light is to avoid the dark, and a love for

summer is a dislike for winter. Thus, the desire and the dislike are as the two sides of a single coin. Both are children of the heart, and frequently the friends of reason.

But fear is an enemy of the heart, and is blind to reason —for it is frequently undirected and without a goal.

Many more have died from fear itself than have ever been killed for want of it.

All fears are hatched from the *was*—and hover as ghosts to haunt the *will be*.

Know that he who has begun to hoard his yesterdays, has nothing with which to build a Now. He is settling himself in the dark and non-existent. He is building himself a tomorrow of fear—largely the fear of death.

Old age is not the passing of youth, but the saving of yesterdays.

But he is young, though his hair be as snow, if he lives in the present and ever finds new pleasures in so living there.

However, it should be recognized that the things which bring our greatest pleasures, cause our greatest griefs.

Without sorrow, there is no pleasure; and without pleasure, there is no sorrow—but without either, there is no life.

Sorrow is the wind that bears pleasure aloft. Pleasure feeds the body, and sorrow is the offal. Pleasure sweeps clean the mind, and sorrow is the sweepings.

Sorrow is the yesterday of pleasure. But pleasure itself is the present, the living *Is*. The basis of all things and all acts, the higher morale—such is pleasure.

Were it not for the joy of living, its urge for creative expression, its song of laughter—then the life that is man would rapidly end itself.

All living things are predicated on pleasure, and they

who would have children must have recourse thereto.

In pleasure lies conception, creativity, the new—whether this be a child, a work of art, or a new idea for today.

It is truly strange that the child should weep at birth—for only the human, of all animals, can laugh.

To the great man, pleasure is the spice of all living. He takes pleasure in the doing, and the work becomes play.

And this defines the hard play of the healthy as against the trudging efforts of the slave—that though both do the same things, the one laughs. He is happy.

Let us live then, and play! Away with work. I have yet to see one thing worthy of the solemnity bestowed even upon a jester.

Relax and enjoy life! They die doubly quick who, to the rush of time, add their own mad pace. And they who concern themselves with what does not concern them, throw life away.

But the men about you look upon all things as serious. They lack the wisdom of laughter.

Truly, all humanity suffers from a great sickness. It is this—they become solemn before they have learned to laugh.

There is a sickness called gravity, and in the delirium that follows, the sorrows of others are also caught.

But I should like to say this—that one cannot breathe for another, and neither can he feel for him. Each has his own life, his own pleasures, and his own sorrows—and he who bears the pleasures or the sorrows of another does so because he is pleased or sorry with himself.

Sorry indeed is he who bears the sorrows of others in order to be sorry for himself.

Whenever you feel grieved by the sorrows of those

about you, remember that the total grief of all the world can be no greater than the greatest grief of one man, and the pleasures of all the world likewise no greater.

In this, you are equal to the whole world. Have I not always said that each was a world within himself?

And I would tell you how to maintain this world, and be happy, for pleasure is recognition of things as they are in the present, for what they are—and wearying oneself not with what they cannot be.

Seek joy in all things—for even the worthless is eternal. What is, simply is. He who grieves about it twists a cord on his own throat.

Happiness and sorrow do not arise from what occurs —but rather, from our opinions of the occurrences. If we are to be happy, then, we must look to ourselves, and not to the world outside.

To change the world outside may not be within our power. But it is within our power not to be disappointed with it, and thereby unhappy.

The wise man is a joyous man because he knows enough about nature to know what *not* to demand of her.

Above all other things, he knows that he must live only in this hour, the present, the point of change. For unless one lives in the present, he will not be in harmony with that which is and must be—and he will be swept into senility.

O my friends! I would have you dance the dance of life in the changing rhythm of the cyclic and eternal *Is*. One cannot stake out his camel and ride in the caravan.

The world within you, and of you, must ever be created anew, with love and laughter, in the light of today's sun!

Let all your truths and all your acts be tempered with laughter. Dip them deep in the pot of joy, white hot!

Behind all creation, all life, sounds this laughter, this echo of eternal order, this drum beat of the rhythm of all things. For the greatest pleasure lies in creation— whether this be the creation of an ideal, a child, or a new world for today.

And what do I say of death, that I laugh?—only this, that it hangs curtains about the present, making it precious after it is late, too late!

Thus spoke Akhnaton, builder of temples, before the assembled nobles in the City of the Horizon.

From the south, and the pleasure lakes of Maru-Aton, came the scent of flowers, and on the same winds the music of tambourines and systrums, mingled with the haunting strains of ancient love songs of Egypt.

And a Nubian slave shaded the Pharaoh's eyes with a large feather fan as the morning sunlight glanced from the vases in the open temple—vases from the islands "of great waters."

And the arms of the lovely Nefertiti slipped about him, and through her thoughts ran words of love.

But the words remained unspoken, for her eyes widened with horror—there was blood on the lips of Akhnaton as he smiled at her!

And the Pharaoh, "he that lived in truth," fell softly to the colored glass pavement of the temple. And the red blood mingled with the mosaic of yellow flowers, blue sky, and the white wings of wild pigeons.

2
Land of the Seven Terraces

Come, sit around me, my friends, and I shall tell you the story of Svetaketu, the grandson of Aruna.[11]

For Svetaketu was a prince, born of the Kshatriyas,[12] the kingly race from beyond the mighty mountains.

White was his skin,[13] as the petals of the sacred lotos, and his strength was that of the elephants which are led from the forests of Himavat.[14] Truly, the fragrance of good fortune swirled about him till none was so beloved in the Land of Seven Terraces.[15]

On a throne built of wishing pearl, sat Prince Svetaketu, in a palace of beryl and crystal, a palace of forty pinnacles which pillared up the ten parts of the sky even like Mount Kailasa[16]—whose sides are bright with colored lines of metal. Here tile mosaics formed the stairs leading to silver pavilions whereon great lotos patterns were inlaid with moonstone.

And the lake of the Land of Seven Terraces was known as the Lake of Colored Lights, and it was encircled with Sinduvara shrubs, palms, and bell-trees—like a lovely bride lying asleep on a pillow of roses.

Into this lake emptied the River of Playing Lutes, the beaches whereof were of gold dust and blue pearls. And from the mists of this river, great music clouds floated over the Land of Seven Terraces, the rain therefrom being perfumed as the mandarava flowers.

24

All things were his—gardens of nutmeg and areca where he watched the dancers from the Temple of the Tortoise, which is in Kalinga[17]—the fragrance of aloes and dark sandalwood, carriages yoked with the spotted deer, and blossoms of amber and coral where nested the wild kokila.

And in the grove of the tamarinds, through which green pigeons flew, were many beautiful women to beg for love beneath canopies of silk and on cushions as soft as the breasts of swans.

Painted were their faces, as with collyrium, their feet stained with red, armlets on their arms, anklets on their ankles, and their hips girdled only by veils.

There they bathed among the water lilies, or mocked the tinkling of the fountains with their tambourines tapped with painted finger tips.

Some of them, with their golden zones tinkling, wandered about making music where they walked, and others sang. One lay asleep, embracing her big lute as if it were a friend, and rolled it about while its strings trembled. And still another, with her hair loose and disheveled, and her skirts and ornaments fallen from her loins, lay like a woman crushed by an elephant and then dropped.

But even among all these pleasures, Svetaketu was dark of heart—dark as he who has eaten of the creeper plant which bears a poison berry.

As the unbaked earthen pot is crushed by the weight of a stone, so pleasure lay heavily upon him, crushing his spirit.

Tears dropped from his eyes, as the mango drips honey from its shaken blossom, and through his breast whipped a fire whose smoke was sighs, whose flame despair.

Thus, there came a day when Svetaketu departed from the Land of Seven Terraces, having traded the red sandalwood of the prince for the red rags of the beggar. The soft breasts of the garden-women he forsook for the rough grass of the ascetic forest.

Many hundreds of yoganas[18] he traveled to the land of Himavat, and finally came upon an ancient scholar who greeted him in this manner:

"Where do you travel, O my son? Yours is the bearing of a lion, yet you carry the wooden alms-bowl of the begging brikshu."[19]

And thus answered Svetaketu, Prince of the Land of Seven Terraces:

I have sickened of the pleasures of the world, and I have left it—hoping to obtain peace.

Wisdom has told me that a man may conquer the world, but still can live in only one house—and of a thousand cloaks, only one may be worn at a time.

All pleasures were mine. But pleasures are as brief as the fruit of the plantain. They are like a torch of hay: it blazes and is gone, almost before it's lighted.

As a fire is never satisfied with fuel, neither is a man satisfied with pleasure. He is ever in want of more—and of this want I have grown weary, for all pleasures were mine.

And when he had heard such words from the lips of one so young, the scholar was filled with pity. And he said to Svetaketu:

It is true that many pleasures are brief—for these are the pleasures of the young, and youth is also brief.

Would you like to know why youth is brief? It is because one tires of the old pleasures, and has not learned to find the new.

Only he grows old who does not allow his pleasures to grow with him.

And this, my son, is the maturity of pleasure—that it becomes wisdom. Truly, this is the ripening and the fruit thereof.

Wisdom is the expansion of the self to encompass new horizons. It is the constant re-creation of the self, and pleasure is inherent in the act—even as in the creation of a child in the body of one's beloved.

Thus, you should look for wisdom, for wisdom is eternal. Never has its source run dry. Many a tree is bare, and many a fruit decayed, but the vines of knowledge are forever fertile, and their fruit forever ripe—and the day of their passing shall not be.

Wisdom is of the ages, but life is of the day. He who does not extend himself with knowledge, sinks with the sunset.

Come, live with me in my cave in the mountains, and I shall tell you of the dance of Shiva[20]—the dance of the eternal *Is*.

Come with me, and I shall tell you of the urge for creation—the flesh and bone of pleasure—which is called love. For it exists in all things, even to the last pebble on the least stream. Knowing these things, you shall gain wisdom, which is in itself the higher pleasure—and you shall again love the world in which you breathe.

A man is made up of what he loves—and he loves that of which he has knowledge—else there would have been no urge to gather this knowledge.

Both liking and disliking, love and hatred, can co-exist with ignorance and lack of understanding. However, only love can grow with the growth of knowledge. And as ignorance disappears, so disappears hatred—to be replaced, even at its worst, by pity or sympathy, the sisters of love. Thus, there is a direct relationship between love and knowledge, and between hatred and ignorance. Among other things, therefore, knowledge opens the door for love.

No one has ever hated that of which he has had complete understanding. Hatred is a shadow before the eyes —cast by the heavy brows of ignorance.

Know that one cannot fight for the love of anything. These terms are self-contradictory. One only fights out of hatred against the opposite of that which he loves. And it is questionable whether hatred has ever yet led to a worthy act. Wise indeed is he to whom the opposite of love is tolerance and sympathy.

So spoke the ancient sage in the forest of Himavat. And his words filled Svetaketu with a strange joy, and he knelt before the aged one and said:

Glad is this day, O my master, for you have come to me as sunlight upon distant hills, and a rainbow after long storms.

To me, your words are a gateway to open roads. They are a banner in the fore, and I shall surely follow after you, wherever you may lead.

Whereupon, Svetaketu took up his life with the sage. And that night, having laid the cave with fresh grass, they dressed in white robes and seated themselves to talk. The stars above glittered like the beads of bright stones in the bed of the Indus, and to these many-eyed heavens the learned one motioned as he said:

Witness the stars above us. Each has a perfect shape. Each moves with a perfect rhythm—both of itself, and among the other stars. They dance the eternal dance of Shiva.

And the earth on which we sit—it has a perfect shape. And it moves with rhythm, bringing the pulsing of day and night. And about the sun it also moves with rhythm, giving and taking the seasons of the year. It dances the eternal dance of Shiva.

Behold yourself, O my Prince—the swinging of your heart, the breathing in and out, even the tread of your feet as you walk from the cave at sun-up! Is not your every movement one of rhythm? Is not your body one of perfect shape? And do you not feel within yourself the urge to dance?

Believe me, O my son, Shiva is not a god. Neither is Shiva a man, or any other creature like unto those known to man. Having no head, and having no body, Shiva is neither matter nor spirit.

Shiva is a word, a name, a symbol—a word for the perfection of order and organization that is present in all existence, a name for the rhythm that is inherent in all that is, a symbol of the dance—the deathless dance of the things that are in the eternal present.

For order, and organization, and rhythm, and life are all one and the same thing seen through different windows in the house of being.

Order is the repetition of like things in space—as the stones that form your palace, O my Prince, or the stars in the heavens above.

Rhythm is the repetition of like things in time—as the moving feet of your dancing girls, the beat of your drums, or the stars in the heavens above.

*Life is the repetition of like things in space and time—their reproduction—*as the child, or the seed of the plant, or the crystal, or the stars in the heavens above.

All these things are the same: Order, Rhythm, Life—and all are Shiva. That which has order moves with rhythm, and the orderly rhythmic thing is living. It dances the eternal dance which gives it being.

Truly, even in the very depths of your mind, O my son, are the dictates of the universe and the rhythm of the stars—for the lowliest habit is no more than a repetition of like acts. It is rhythm in itself.

And as are the habits of man, so is his society—for all societies are likewise built upon the repetition of like acts, called customs, traditions, and rituals. They are rhythm in themselves.

This is that which is called life. It is the dance of Shiva making itself known in space and time, in the tangible and the intangible, in the stone, and the man, and his thought alike.

This is that which arises from the *Rita*[21]—those immutable ordinances which are inherent in and maintain the existence of all matter, even to the last dust-mote in the last out-post of space.

Because of the Rita, the everlasting rhythm of matter, one part of matter can interact with another, man can live, and the universe can pulse with the order of endless cycles.

And I would make known to you an even greater truth, O Svetaketu! I would tell you that the Rita (those vast and ubiquitous laws of universal rhythm and order) maintain the existence of all things by bringing about their continuous self-creation, a constant renewing, an eternal building-up, a re-creation and well-spring of joy—the urge for creation which is inherent in all that is, and which is known in man by the term of *love*.[22]

And I ask you, what is love? And you will say, that which the mother has for the child, the horse for its off-spring, the cow for its calf, yes, even the swine for the pigs thereby.

And I ask again, what is love? And you will further reply that it is some intangible law which knits together the male and his mate, and thereby gives rise to creation, to the reproduction or repetition of like-kind—as indeed they must be like-kind, for the father denies the child with the face of another.

It is indicative of the absolute order and rhythm of man, that in his societies *the unlike is the dislike*.

But this do I say to you—that the Rita makes possible this repetition of like-kind. It is the eternal dance of Shiva. Many other names does it have. In space, it is called order. In time, it is called rhythm. In music, it is called harmony. In human behavior, it is called habit. In human cultures, it is called customs, social organization, rites, and rituals. But in the basis of life itself, it is love, reproduction, and the urge for creation. And in all of this—whether it be man or music—it is the same Rita, the same drums beating the universal dance of Shiva.

Even as the universe maintains its existence as a body through continuous self-creation and the building up of matter, and the rhythm of its deathless cycles, so does the human body maintain its existence through continuous self-creation, and the race of man likewise through the repetition of like-kind. And why, I ask, should we assume that there is more than one Rita, one dance of Shiva, seeing that all these are the same, and that man himself is suckled of the dust and stone of earth?

Why, then, are you heavy of heart? Are you not a child begotten of the earth by the rhythm of the universe? You are of the flesh and bone of earth, and to her you return in the everlasting cycle of being.

The very salt of the sea, which hatched our life, still laps the shores of the body in the rhythmic brine of blood. The heat of the sun is in our hearts, and the stones of earth in our bones.

Truly, you are a child of the earth—yes, and a creation of like-kind, not only in being, but also in mind. Do you doubt that man is the son of the universe, and that he is, in mind, a creature of like habits?

Note the thoughts of man! Even as nature herself, everything he does is done with order—for he cannot remember nor understand that which is laid before him without order. And even as nature, when he tears down that which is built, he does so only to create that which he sees in his own heart as a greater order.

Witness the works of man, and the habits of man, and the customs of his societies—for man cannot gather to himself that which is without order, nor can he recognize that which is without order, and every act wherein he acts bears the stamp of the mind—yes, the stamp of the universe, his father, which is order and rhythm and their creation.

The simplest processes of his body, his most primitive homes, his earliest dances, his first music—do not these bear the heaviest and closest order and rhythm, the repetitive roll of the drums? Was he not thereby closer to earth and simpler in his habits and customs?

Long have I shrunk from those who would deny man his great heritage—that he was born to the earth from the love of the universe, his father.

Love has many names for its many manifestations. It is called pattern, order, the urge to create, harmony, and rhythm. But it is all of these, and many yet unknown—for it is the *Rita*, the dance of Shiva.

The gold in your right hand, the stone in your left—their material basis is the same. It is only their internal organization and order which make these what they are. Otherwise, they would be the same, and so would you.

Watch the artist busy at his sketches. Why do he and a thousand others work in a labor of love, through darkness and poverty, caring not for money or fame? Is it not that they are creating, begetting the new?

Safely may you lift your hand against the artist, but speak not against his work. He has fathered these children. He loves them.

The filling of the belly gives satisfaction—but the creative urge alone gives joy, whether the conception is that of child or a work of art. It is from this universal well that the libations of natural pleasure pour forth.

And yonder flowers along the stream—in the growth that brought their blossoms, they found their death. Yet they could not hesitate. They followed the Rita. They danced the eternal dance of Shiva in the reproduction of like-kind—so often called love.

Every flower is an expression of universal love—and every seed is its evidence.

And even as the flowers, and even as man, so do the heavens repeat themselves in being day and night, light of the moon and dark, and winter and summer, the sowing and the reaping—for all things have a rhythm and move in cycles. And it is this which is known as the dance of Shiva.

O my son! There is pleasure in order—in its straight-

ness and its curves and the music of its symmetry. There
is joy in its creation, in the making and the seeing. And
there is joy in its rhythm—in the rhythm of the heart,
and the dance, and the laugh. Who but smiles at the
rhythm of children's feet, or thrills to the pulsing of
drums?

Are not this rhythm and this order the structure of the
universe itself, and inherent within all matter? And is it
not inherent within you also—being as you are, a special
matter fashioned by the universe?

Do you not feel the urge to dance? Is not man the most
rhythmic of all creatures—and does he not thereby also
possess the greatest order, and the greatest mind, and
the greatest works?

I read me into a book. I listen to the words of Shiva.
Love came as a rhythm, and the rhythm had the shape
of order, and all things danced into life!

The pulsing of the stars became the pulsing of the
heart, and the waxing and the waning of the moon fixed
the waiting hours of women. But, as the youth and age
of a man, so are the spring and autumn seasons—and the
earth moves on.

Fill yourself with joy! Laugh with me! Step the varied
rhythmic measure in the dance of all that is!

Eternal is the order and the rhythm of that which is
without—and eternal also that within yourself. Be it the
dance of the waves or the beat of the heart, the same
drums are singing the roll!

Thus spoke the ancient scholar in the forests of Himavat, and the heart of Svetaketu grew light in his breast.
All grief departed from him—like a great black bird which

lifts its wings and flies away, leaving behind the lotos it had hidden.

The three dark clouds of old age, sickness, and death became as mists and faded—now seen through by a sharper eye.

A love for pleasure surged up within him, an urge to dance, and he turned to the ancient one in wonder—but lo! He had vanished! There seemed to be a rolling of drums, and in his stead, the garden women danced to the music thereof!

Bubbles of light floated through the sky as stars, a shower of heavenly mandarava flowers fell about him, and the flute-voices of wild birds sounded in the rose-apple groves of the garden.

Two great mountains reared their heads on either side, and in the midst of the valley made thereby, a white fountain burst into laughter, and the waters of the fountain grew into a river which emptied into a broad and peaceful lake.

And lo! Svetaketu saw that it was the Lake of Colored Lights in the Land of Seven Terraces! Beyond the lake, white as the swans that swam thereon, stood the Palace of Forty Pinnacles!

Prince Svetaketu sprang up from the gold-dust beach with arms outstretched, and cried aloud:

"It was Shiva! It was Shiva! He has spoken to me—even as he laid his hand upon the dancing waters!"

But she who had lain beside her prince, lovely as the morning sun, was troubled, and said:

"Shiva?—but there has been no one here other than ourselves! You were dreaming, O my Prince, though I know not whence came this wooden begging bowl—and behold yourself in the water! You are wearing the rags of a Brikshu!"

3

Millenniums of the Lordly Stars

And it came to pass that we beheld Alborz,[23] the mother of mountains, and a fountain of light—and the fountain splashed about her veins of gold as though the veins were cut.

Thitherward we journeyed, on the way of the light, and beyond, to a place near Barda. And lo! Before us lay a city walled with mountains![24]

Beautiful was the city, and in the midst thereof, and to the south, a deep lake whose throat was stone opened into seven streams.

A fire-temple reared its dome into the mountains, and we saw that it was topped with silver and a crescent. Porphyry columns upheld its roof, and everything was rich with fret-work of gold.

And a voice spoke to us, saying: "Witness the city of Afrasyab, the Turanian![25] Feast your eyes upon it, and say if there is any like it in all the many regions of the earth!"

And we looked, and found it lovely as all of man's desires. Jasper fountains in the garden flowed into marble tanks wherein the gold fish swam among the lotos flowers.

Almonds and aloes waved their silvery sprays, and in the branches of the pomegranate tree, the wild sun-bird nested and laid its eggs of mottled grey.

Pink oleanders and whispering pipal boughs caressed

the enameled cupolas of the palace of a hundred columns, and from this palace the voice again cried out:

It is I—Khizer, the immortal! It was I who gave the cup to Hafiz of Shiraz!

Listen to my words, and I shall tell you of the *mahin cherkh*,[26] the great cycle wherein all things are eternal —even as myself who dwell in that eternal day, the present.

In the beginning, all things were—for there was no beginning, just as there shall be no end. Find me the corner of a circle, and then shall I say, truly, you were right, there is a beginning.

Only when I have seen the first of life and the last of man, will I admit that the line between these points is straight.

"But," you will say, "is this not a starting and a finishing—that the day and year beginning, and the day and year ending, can be reckoned?"

No, my children, your mistake is this—that you should think these things to be. Does the earth stop in her spinning that you may reckon with her?

Day and year are only names, and a naming of names. Yesterday was today, and today shall be tomorrow—and should you doubt, ask the blind to note the sunset.

Do not let your days be named, as evening, Tuesday, summer. Do not limit them with the curtains of ancient error and the connotations of the past. Each is new, and each is old, and each is eternal—but only insofar as you yourself live in the present.

Only the present, this day, and they who live within the day, are existing and eternal.

As is the farthest star, so is the sun, and so is the earth, and so is the smallest particle of matter—all are spinning bodies. All move in eternal and indestructible orbits. Cycles within cycles, cycles about cycles—they are smaller than the eyes can see or the mind conceive, and equally so are they larger—and their counting is beyond the dreams.

Thus, one who lives upon the earth—a spinning body within a spinning system—can see nothing in its entirety. All things are known only in phases. And as one cannot know all time, neither can he see all space. And for this reason, my children, you speak of beginning and end.

You live in the *mahin cherkh*, the great cycle. But the short of sight say, "whence I came—that is the beginning. As far as I can see—that is the end."

But any circle great enough appears straight to him who has a short view of it, even as the earth appears flat for the same reason. And because of this, many men believe in the death of all things.

Yes, you can find a beginning and an end of *parts* of nature. But nature is a whole, and a continuum. It has no parts except those that are of your own thinking.

He who cuts nature into parts fashions these parts to fit his own standards, his ideas of like and dislike, good and bad, and beginning and end.

There is a vast circle called life. Man draws a mark thereon, and says: "Here is birth—so begins the cycle. And here is death—and so it ends." But cycles have no beginning and end save when they are marked as such. And tell me—who is man that he should draw marks on all existence?

Who has returned to those recognizing him, after death, and spoken of the finality of all things? And what voice has broken through what unknown curtain, before the body is born, speaking of an absolute beginning?

Man has a birth—can he remember it? Man shall cease

to breathe—can he name the time? He cannot. And yet, he would point to these as beginning and end!

Man knows only of his existence in the Here and Now, the living day—but he wastes much of this worrying about the non-existent, including his yesterday and tomorrow.

Of life and death no man knows more than that he *is,* and that he is *now.* All else is conjecture—and of these there may be many.

So I declare it—that you never can know death because you can never be living-dead. These are different realms through which your cycle rolls.

When you exist, death is a part of the still non-existent future. And when you are dead, you can know nothing of it. Death, then, is unimportant either to those who live or to those who do not live.

Death is not the opposite of life. Non-existence is the opposite of life—and also the opposite of death.

That which exists, exists. That which is unreal, is unreal. One can never change into the other. Realize, O my children, that there is not one hair of proof for these statements of beginning and end. But for the living, and the present, there is proof in you yourself.

Fear not that your shadow lengthens in the evening. The day comes. The day goes. But the earth rolls on— for she has neither come nor gone. And throughout all time, it is the same day, the eternal present. And so it is with all things, including you.

Fear not that your shadow lengthens. Your sun has not set, nor can it set—for you are not unreal and a name, like "day" or "year." You are flesh and bones suckled of the dust and stone of earth itself—and like unto her of whom you are a part, you continue your cycle through existence.

Fear not. Your sun cannot set. You have merely been

carried beyond its light. And as the earth makes day and night by her spinning, so does the universe make similar names "life" and "death" for you—by the very laws whereby you first were born.

There are no miracles not ordained by nature, worked by her, and in her cause. The coming and going of the sun of the day and the moon of the night are miracles. And your coming and going shall be a like miracle—and no less surprising.

For this do I say to you—that there is nothing that does not obey natural laws in its every motion. And such is a law of nature, that all things move in cycles and are rhythmic in the eternal order of all that is. Therefore, nothing that truly exists can cease to exist forever.

The laws of the universe are the only established truths, and they are the only laws of justice. And I ask you—if death were justice, what could be said of injustice?

For awhile you shall be darkness and dust, and less than dust. But grieve not that this should be so. The heart that bore poetry at the sight of summer morning, the sound of singing bird, the beat of autumn rain, shall become a part of that morning, that song, that rain.

Forever onward rolls the wheel of being, and the rhythm of its rolling is the drums of Shiva, beating an eternal dance.

The rhythm of your heart is the rhythm of the dance of the stars—even unto their smallest mote of light. The coming and the going of the summer, and the day of the summer, is the rhythm of the spheres and the pulsing of musical strings. All these, and all else that you might behold, have their pulsing—their coming and going. Why then, will you not admit it of yourself? Would you be he alone who stands silent in the eternal dance of all that is?

Is there, within you, no urge to dance? Are you a stranger to the world, that there is no laughter in your heart, no throbbing of the drums? And if there is, dance then, and laugh—you who are most rhythmic of all creatures, you who dwell within the everlasting present. Let it be known that you are a part of the universe, and alive thereby!

When a song is sung, only one note is heard at a time —yet the song is there. Sing, then, this note of the Now in the vast and rhythmic symphony of the eternal.

And why should you fear to spend tomorrow with your mother, the earth? Have you in any way offended her? Furrows of pain have you plowed across her breast—yet she has not scolded.

In a mother's eyes are all children the same. Your mother, the earth, is no woman-of-the-market—you cannot buy of her.

Naked are you born, and naked take your bed again; for great is the king, and small the fool, but their bones are all the same.

Behold the universe, in which are all things! As a great sphere is the universe, a curve that has no end, and the "parts" of which can have no end, and like unto which there is no other.

Turn your eyes to the universe, the unbegotten. Forever has it been. And it shall be—forever.

A dust-mote in the sunbeam of time—you call it earth, the abode of man. It dances in, it dances out, and the sunbeam knows it not.

Lo! The dust-mote rears a thing called man, a creature of many whims and many creeds. But I say unto you, whatever be your creed, whatever be your idol, the universe knows it not.

The creeds of man are many, and a breeding of many wars, yet there is no man but is blessed of the earth he curses. Each bends his head in wonder before the lordly stars—his god of a day forgotten.

In the night of time, earth reared her child, her one of choice, and mother love possessed her. And the infant blessed the soil that suckled him. He raised his eyes to the fiery sun, giver of light. He stood in wonder beneath the lordly stars and breathed in their glory.

And the first-born built a temple to the fire—to Atar, the dancing fire that symbolizes the energy and rhythm that is life and the sun. He studied the wanderings of the great stars, and made sacred the laws of the universe. Thus began the earliest faith.

But this do I declare—that these later faiths which set times of beginning and ending, these creeds that transgress the laws of the universe, are written in a childish scrawl and still bear the limitations of the human mind.

The universe has no beginning or end. It bears within itself that which is called time. Know, O my friends, that you are a part of the universe. You also bear within yourselves that which is called time.

You cannot pass into eternity, for you are already in it.

In a dreamless sleep, an ocean of eternity does not equal the drip of a water-clock.

Time is yours, and of your making. One hour in the life of a youth is longer than the longest day of the aged one.

Do the aged, then, hasten ever faster to their deaths, that their days seem shorter? Ah no—the length of time is still the same, and the Now is just as interesting—but they have lost interest in it. Their present and their life thereby escape them.

Interest in the Here, and attention to the Now, is a

longness of days and a longingness of life—for such is the essence of youth.

Believe me, O my children, there is no difference between the finite and the infinite—and the apparent difference is only the scar of human limitation.

You are already in and a part of the infinite and eternal. There is no when, before, and after—no yesterday or tomorrow. There is only today, the everlasting present, the pulsing cycle of the Now.

This small, my friends, is time—that within the breadth of a thought you can span eternity.

One thought, the dust of a second, is all you have or can hope to have—only the great fire of the eternal present lighting up your circle of being as it rolls out of the nonexistent future into the non-existent past.

Would you deny that the circle exists—merely because there will come a time when you can no longer see the light? Is not the universe of which you yourselves are a part, spherical?—and do not all things move in cycles and with the perfect rhythm of the dance of Shiva?

Would you deny that the circle exists? Are you afraid that tomorrow morning will not come merely because, following sunset, the earth has rolled into the darkness?

The only manner in which the universe can maintain itself is by its complete and perfect cyclic motion. Thereby is it stable and eternal. If transcience or instability of the universe were possible, it would have been reached long since, and man would be dead, and all activity stilled, and you and I would not be here to do the things we do.

But lo! Here is man, and here is activity, and all the things that are. And only one thing could have made it so—the fact that it is a world of perfect order, perfect balance, perfect rhythm—which are manifested in the perfect cycles that make you, and you, and you, my friends, eternal.

You are a part of the universe, and of the same substance. How can the total universe be orderly and eternal, then, if you or any of its other parts be transient and ephemeral?

He who knows the *mahin cherkh,* the great cycle, lives on both sides of the dawn, the darkness and the light, and thereby also on both sides of the sunset—though he may know it not.

Great indeed are the regions of time—but equally great is the mind of man, for herein also lies infinity and eternity.

In the furthest depths of space, a new sun bursts into being. In the mind of man, a new thought is born. Both are children of the same system of laws, and neither is independent of the other.

But truly, there shall come a day when the sun shall burn low, and the fire shall flicker out. Prepare yourself well for that winter of time, that evening of the worlds when you may step no more in the path of the light, like Yima, southward on the way of the sun. Then shall the winds sweep down from the mountains bringing the final snow.

Many star-years past, the great cold descended, and the sun burned out and smiled down no more. In that ancient writing of our fathers, the *Rig,* it is recorded.

It is recorded by the ancients that the earth shall turn for many millenniums. Then shall come the great winter ending the season of being. But know in your own hearts, there shall be a glorious spring—even as there has always been.

As the rain becomes snow, falling deep and white, I would remind you that water is the most formless of all substances. No drop thereof keeps its identity for long. Soon it falls to the earth, mixes with the rivers, and then becomes a part of the ocean whence life itself first came.

Upon your right, upon your left, will be this formless water—and you will call it snow. Yet there will be no flake thereof but will be different, with a perfect form, and a delicate shape, though these number as the leaves of all trees or the sands of all shores.

Know in your own hearts that, as is the snow, so is the water—and that order and rhythm and form are inherent in all things existing, and that they cannot be destroyed.

Let this snow, then, which shall herald the darkness, be an omen and a promise of the springtime which shall come.

And having so spoken, and so prophesied, the voice of the immortal Khizer wandered, then seemed to break into some ancient and unknown chant:

O children of the light! I entreat you, discard your bladder-rattles! Throw down your idol-houses! Place no faith in hymns to super-earthly things!

Many are the idol-makers, but how many more carry their idols within!

You who are pregnant with an idol within, bent are your backs, and your brows tracked with pain—for you are heavy with a stone. Cast it out, or it will crush you under!

You who are heavy with an idol—cast it out! For the hours of your labor shall be many, and all idols are still-born.

Wherefore are you dissatisfied with your mother, the earth, and what she has to offer? Listen, and I shall tell you.

He who is dissatisfied has a cause and a reason. Sick is he, and delirious, for he raves of things that are not, nor cannot be.

You who are sick in mind and heart—confess your sorrows unto your mother, the earth. Does not the lost child need the attention of a mother?

You who are sick in mind and heart—you have wronged your mother, the earth. Go unto her and confess. And of what have you been guilty? Listen, and I shall tell you.

You have built and sacrificed to an idol of wealth and greed. You have placed an image in the temple of the dancing flame—and an even heavier idol in your hearts. You have listened to the words of whisperers and false priests, and have forsaken her commandments.

In this fashion, speak the whisperers: "Lo! The earth is only dust. You can kick it with your feet. Forsake the earth and think of higher things—though you cannot see them, they are there. As the winds of the plains are these higher things, invisible but strong."

O, you sufferers! Thus did you learn to measure with a mental mist! Thus are you nearing madness for want of that which is not!

O, you sufferers! Thus have you sucked milk from the breasts of a she-wolf! Bitter is it, and poison—more bitter than the wormwood, more poison than the nightshade. Spew it forth, and wash your mouth with the milk of your mother, the earth—she has not forsaken you.

Would you sell your goods for coins without a stamp, coins of which you can say nothing? You would not. And yet you would barter your sanity and your life for a whisper and a wind! Is this not the judgment of a fool?

A fool is he who would sell his goods for coins without a stamp, but an even greater fool is he who trades his life for that which is not.

Small is the race of man, and meagre his knowledge. All he knows or can hope to know comes of measurements with standards of his own choosing. If his standards are vapours, his measurements are even less, and his life in this world is the journey of a ghost.

Make known unto me any animal other than man, of which it can be said: "Behold, it lives a life of misery!" You cannot, for there are no such other animals. All animals, except man, are happy—and except where they have known man and his ways!

Of all animals, man alone has denied the laws of the earth, seeking to live wholly by laws of his own—and of all animals, he is thereby most miserable.

Those creatures thrive best, and are happiest, who understand no more than nature taught them.

Only man has exceeded the bonds of nature without yet having understood nature itself.

These are the sick ones, the dissatisfied who expect earth to change to fit their dreams of things that are not.

O you sufferers! You sick of heart! Return to your mother, the earth, and confess. She has not forsaken you. Super-earthly things are but ribbons for a dream, veils for a marriage of sunbeams.

Within the bedroom of a thought, the giddy moon is ravished; and he that casts his seed into the belly of a cloud will be a father unto seven ogres—all of which will differ.

I beg of you, O my brothers, lust not after super-earthly things. Fair may be the creature of your dreams, lovelier than the lily of the valley. But pass her by—for she will rear you a devil.

Though the milk of her breasts is sweet, it is poison. Though her skin be soft as the rose, touch it not. Carry your seed elsewhere—for she will rear you a devil.

Fair may be the creature of your dreams, more lovely than Shirin,[27] mistress of Khosru, the Defier of Allah. But though she live in a palace of forty thousand columns of silver and plated wood, touch her not—for she will rear you a devil.

Fairer than Laili[28] may be the creature of your dreams, with eyes as dark as the waters of Amoo,[29] with breasts as white as the beating wings of midnight moths, with legs that curl on the satin like the snow-lit tresses of Zal[30] —but take yourself from her bed. For those who ravish a corpse bring back the smell of the dead.

He that casts his seed into the belly of a cloud will be a father unto seven ogres, and thus shall he bemoan his fate: "Wretched me! What have I done! Through these veins, once bright with fire, swirls an alien dust, and it grates the bone of me!"

He that cuts his teeth in the night-wind of super-earthly things, shall grow to lust after them. He shall return to be drained of his youth, and his bones shall become hard and dusty as those which worms have long since left, and the house of his heart shall be a ruins.

O my brothers! Like all other things, love is eternal. But it is more than this—for it is an arbor whereon the vine of life entwines its way to the sun. But lo! He who is in love with shadows builds an arbor of these, and his is the vine which crawls upon the stones and bears a bitter fruit. Unto shadows only shadows can cling.

There shall be a day when each shall have dust upon his eyes. But those who seek after the visions of the desert have dust in their hearts—the dry-rot of a shadow world!

Thus spoke Khizer,[31] the immortal, in the city known

as Shiz—the city of Afrasyab the Turanian. And as he spoke of dust, behold! The city became dust!

Green mould crept across the brass doors of the four great gateways, and the arches crumbled, and the walls fell away—leaving not even a mound where once the mighty city stood breathing in the morning sunlight.

And all things died—even the budded lily which floated on the bosom of the lake. Khizer was gone.

Only to the immortal are all things immortal.

4

The Peach-blossom Fountain

When the sun burns low in the evening lands, and the sightless eyes of night gaze across deathless China, Tao Chien[32] dreams of the Peach-blossom Fountain.

Deep in the bamboo grove, Tao Chien rides up to paradise on the dream-crane, while moon-shadows weave the forget-sorrow grass into strange patterns.

The nine celestial spheres wheel overhead, and night comes to the Peach-blossom Fountain, the garden the fisherman found—night, more peaceful than the life of the immortals in the jade green sea.

Up the Flower River, from the bamboo grove, through the fire-fly caves, there lies the Peach-blossom Fountain.

There grow the wu-tung trees where sing the mango birds. There hides the wild mi-deer, and the golden love-pheasant builds her nest.

There the great cold never reaches, never the flap of the snow-goose through the clouds, and from the river's edge no sound of the beating of cold weather robes.

The seals and tassels of office are forgotten, forgotten the pendant badge of rank, the green official coat.

Peace, only peace—and the dreams of Tao Chien, unbroken by the rattle of fish-skin war-drums, or the grind of sharpening sword.

Peace in the bamboo grove, and Tao Chien dreams of paradise. And through the dream, music like moving water sounds.

Silver finger-guards sweep over the twelve brass strings of the cheng.[33] Reed pipes send out the multi-colored notes of the song of "Rainbow-skirt and Feather-jacket."

Upon the sleepy river, duck-weed blossoms into lotos, and along the bank, smart-weed bears wild chrysanthemum flowers.

The painted birds which flap their wings on the slatted screen with every breeze, change to dancing flower-girls posturing the wu dance.

Tao Chien smiles in his dream. More delicate than the paintings of Mao Yen Shou,[34] than the figures in ancient porcelain, this dance—the whirling pheasant-feather fans, the hair heavy with golden birds, hairpins of jade!

Tao Chien smiles. Not since the Lady Li[35] had there been such dancing, such beauty!

Then, and from far away, roll the drums of the Dragon-chant, and the dream shifts. It is the feast of "Passing-over-the-year."

Tao Chien sees the scarlet red-pepper dish, redder still in the light of the man-fish candles. And dressed in the open-work gauze of Yueh, the flowered brocade of Shu, he sits down to a magnificent dinner.

Rhinoceros-horn chop-sticks lift shining fish from crystal clear platters, fragrant keng rice, Golden City native curds, Chang-an winter pickles, frosted pears, bitter dates, and iced syrup served in a jade green bowl.

Tao Chien is at paradise, and the clear wine of "enlightened men" flows freely in and out of the beaten metal cups.

All is happiness, more happiness than at Lo Yu Yuan. Then, outside—and again from far away—the wail of the midnight gibbon!

Tao Chien is startled. "The spirit-screen!"[36] he cries

in his sleep, "The spirit-screen—they have pulled it from the door!"

But it is too late! The picture fades: gone the dancing girls, gone the feast. Where sang the mango birds, now cries the lonely crane. Where waved the forget-sorrow grass, now pours the yellow dust of the Sha-Mo desert—dust more yellow than a river reed in autumn!

Tao Chien now beholds himself in a polished disk, leaning on the thorn-staff of old age, clad in the rice-straw hat and cotton robes of the masses.

Thus stands Tao Chien. Underfoot is smart-weed, and in his heart the frost of an early winter. Deep is his misery, deep as a first love broken—and he makes his way to the river's edge.

But lo! Before him is an aged one dressed in the blue cloak of the scholar, and wearing the five-strand beard of the sage. Thus, in the dream, speaks the aged one:

O Tao Chien! Would you, then, give up to the fishes a mind which can behold a paradise?

That which you see is only that which you see—and to another it will always be different. So it is with all things, for they are as they are seen to be, and not otherwise.

Therefore, this world is your world, peculiar to you, and it lives as you live—for no two people live in the same world. Each is a universe to himself.

Even as you are a part of this ocean, this sky, these flowers—in brief, this world—are they not also a part of you, their images in your eyes, your brain? And do they not find their existence in you, insofar as you yourself exist?

Know, O my son, that all things are you, and beyond you there is nothing—insofar as you exist.

The Peach-blossom Fountain which you envisioned, was not the dwelling of the immortals, but only a few hours of your youth returned to your memory.

And why should you be grieved by the years which have passed? Truly, youth is lost only to him who has closed his mind to the present—and this is the beginning of death.

He who has begun to wish for youth is too old to attain it—for he is already in the past wishing for the present.

He who searches for a reason to live might well save his time. He has none.

Forsake not the present, O my son. But should you grow weary with the world, and sickened with what you believe to be the pettiness of man, then rest yourself before going on. Remember, it is always your privilege to seek retreat within yourself.

Small indeed is that mind wherein a man can no longer hide himself.

And if you are lonely, then the loneliness is of you. For only he who has become a stranger unto himself can be a stranger unto others.

He who is a brother to today's sun, and is a true child of the earth, shines upon all alike, and even warms the passer-by. In his smile is their longing, and in his day is their childhood, and his relation to all men is greater than the bonds of blood between any men.

Have you need of a paradise? Behold! You carry it with you, and know it not!

And why should you mix yourself with the fishes—or even those who inhabit the market-place? Can you not, in your own mind, meet and walk with the master, Kung,[37] or sport with the Lady Li?

The cup is half full, or the cup is half empty—so are

the hearts of those who judge their cups of life accordingly.

You are your own universe, wherein time does not exist. But many need a chart—and thereamong is he who has lost his youth.

A man is no more than his thoughts,[38] and thus, no older than he believes himself to be. Many are the youthful who carry the thorn-staff of old age—yes, and many the grey beards who are young.

When I ask, "how old?"—speak not to me of years, for time has little in common with the age of a man. The young of heart are ever young, and the age of a man is reckoned not in years.

White hair may show the passing of years, but it does not tell how they passed—or how much youth went with them.

And if a man has made wise use of his present, he may be young in years, and young at heart—and nonetheless be old in hours.

This also would I have you know—that the passing years do not make wise men. They only make old men. And there is nothing more pitiful than the old man who has nothing but his years to prove his length of life.

Behold! At the Peach-blossom Fountain grew the multi-colored grasses, the grasses of your youth. Yet they are the same as those whereon you now stand. They are for the seeing, but the blind trend them under.

There sang the plaintive winds—the winds of your youth. But they are the same winds which now ruffle your hair. They are for the hearing, but the deaf stumble on.

The odors of undying flowers haunted the Peach-blossom Fountain, soft were the mosses, and the waters fresh wines to your tongue—but the senses of many men are diseased. Their deaths begin early—for they are the ones who have lost their youth.

Late in youth dies the spirit of many men, and in many more it was still-born.

When growth ceases, decay sets in, and death stalks in its tracks.

But of growth there are many kinds. And though there comes a day when the body gets no taller, it is constantly re-creating itself so long as it lives. So must the mind also grow and keep pace with the present by continuously re-creating itself.

The mind that ceases to expand and learn and grow, soon dies—and it kills the body also.

Each of us is the cause of our own aging, our embroiling ourselves in needless cares, our forsaking the simple goods of the earth.[39]

The mind which makes no effort to stay abreast of the present, like a boat with furled sails, drifts further and further back with the current. Into the past it floats, living in yesterday, feeding on memories. But, O my son, this yesterday, this past, is non-existent. Thus does the mind become non-existent. Thus does it slay itself.

The only growth of the mature mind and the mature heart lies in dancing the liquid measure of the present.[40] Nothing is static. Everything waxes and wanes in the rhythm of eternal cycles.

Those who live in the past become as weights about the throats of those who live in the present, tending to drag them under. Note how eagerly the aged hasten to deny to others the youth that is no longer theirs to deny.

Not because joy dies, is old age so often pitiful and a shrinking within—but because hope dies. For hope is the shadow of determination. It is an opener of roads in the urge for creation.

Hope is the shadow of determination—the determination to build, yes, to re-create oneself.

A great hope quickens the heart of even the dying—for he who carries such a hope within his breast senses his mission, and he knows wherein the universe still has need for him.

Old age is not death catching up with life. It is only the hole wherein we bury our hopes.

The summers of man are counted. He lives a score of years, and spends two score ten in dying. And this is a sign of his passing, an omen: that the sunlight has lost its color, and the wind its music—that necessity takes the place of honor, and habit the place of pride—that lust uproots love, and hope grovels in the pit so created.

Where goes the wonderment, the enthusiasm, and the curiosity of youth? Do they die with the aging body? Ah, no—for these are qualities of mind. First they are strangled, and then the body ages for want of them.

O Tao Chien! Why do you not choose to stay youthful, to live with hope, and thus forever possess for yourself the paradise you saw?

A man is no more than his thoughts. If he dwells in the past, he becomes past. But if he dwells in the present, he must confront the problems of the present, and he will live and think as the youths who have no past—for he is young.

A man is no more than his thoughts—even as the universe is no more than the Here and Now. If he would stay young, he must be in harmony with the living present, for only by such harmony, such rhythm, does spring return to the earth.

When you dance the rhythm of the present, then shall you find it to be the dance of youth, the eternal spring. You are at peace with the soil, and the dust of your ancestors shall bless your feet. Truly, the rhythm of the living present is the rhythm of love—and beyond this rhythm, this dance, this order, these eternal cycles, there is nothing.

Such is the rhythm of all things. But lo! Though the universe is orderly, and the soil is orderly, and the things of the soil are orderly, your thoughts are a chaos of shadows, and shadows of shadows!

You are not happy because you cannot understand the world about you—and you cannot understand it because you have ceased to be a part of it in its present hour, and neither have you claimed it for your own.

Would you be happy? Would you be wise? Know, then, that you are seed of the earth. Learn the wishes of your mother, the earth, for these are wishes for your well-being.

To know the rhythm of the universe, the dance of the eternal *Is*, will be to live in harmony with that which gave you birth, guided your childhood steps, and shall rock you peacefully to sleep—as a mother's hand on the crib in the long lasting night.

To pulse with the rhythm of the present is to be at peace with life, secure in the causes of the things that are.

This paradise you seek—you carry it with you. It is power of self, knowledge of self, perfection of self. Who is stronger than he who reads the stars?

Secure in the eternal cycle of things, he can have no fear. Knowing the causes, he can never be angry. Wise in the wishes of the universe, he can never want nor be grieved.

O my son! In man there is a part of the stars, and in man there is a part of the dust, and in man there is the universe—but many, far too many, see only their own back-yard, or that of their neighbor.

The order that is man, and the mind of man, is the same order, the same rhythm, that controls the whole of things. It is the dance of Shiva, the law of love—but in what law book may we read this?

Strike a note on the cheng, and in another room another cheng will pulse and answer with the selfsame note. Why does it answer? They are in harmony with each other, being of like order and like rhythm.

So would I have you be in harmony with the universe that is the present. I would have you pulse, as the cheng —and sing, as the cheng, with the everlasting Now. If you move into the dance of Shiva, if you are in rhythm with the universe, the very stones will laugh with you, the sun and winds will tell you the tales they tell the youth, and the flowers will bear them witness.

Rich in rags is he who knows the dust on which he walks, wise in learning beyond all scrolls, for in this dust also lies the secret of youth, and of love—the heritage of youth.

What can he lack who knows himself to be a part of all things—without beginning, and timeless? Does he not already have all things?

What truths will he be unable to appreciate—he who knows the order of things, and himself a part thereof? Are not the things no more than their order? And is he not also this order?

What hatred can he have, what jealousy, what anger, when he is a part of all causes and effects?

O Tao Chien! From the dust-mote to the star, all things are in harmony with the rhythmic laws of eternal order—and only he who is also in harmony therewith, only he may return to the Peach-blossom Fountain.

Would you feed yourself to the fishes—you who carry a living dream, a paradise with you?

Tell me, wherein lies the difference between the dream and the reality? Both have the same origin, both are conjured up within the brain, and both fade out with the flight of time.

To dream of better things, and to believe in these dreams, and to act upon them, is just as good as to have the things. The wall between the reality and the image thereof is truly thin. It is only a veil of thought.

Thoughts themselves are realities, being just as real as the individual who gave them their existence. And they frequently outlive him.

A man is no more than his thoughts—and the words that are spoken are never heard, and the words that are written are never read. One may only sit in the private theater of his own mind, and watch the drama of his own thoughts—brought about by the words.

Thus, he who wishes to be understood for the man he is, must first appear so to himself. People do not see what we are. They see what we appear to be—and even this frequently is not what we appear to ourselves.

Each of us carries a separate universe within himself, being himself a universe. Each of us created this universe out of the sunlight of childhood's curiosity and the urge for creation. It should throb with the rhythm of love— being, as it is, our child of mind.

If yours is a world of sorrow, strife, unreality, and disillusionment—then yours also is the carpenter's task of rebuilding. But be not dismayed. In the building there is joy, and the urge for creation is fulfilled.

He who rebuilds his life, and re-creates his today,

performs no greater miracle than does mother nature every April of her springtime.

Let us build, then, with stones of "that-which-is" a wall against the storm, a cheerful hearth to warm the years, and a floor on which to dance.

Let us build—but with stones of the earth. All the grief that is man's, whatever be his age, comes of the differences between the world of which he dreams and the world in which he lives. Dream, then, but build a terrestrial world.

Be unto yourself as the universe is unto itself—complete in its being, orderly in its ways, beautiful in its truths, rhythmic in its laughter and its dance.

Do not allow your mind to turn in upon itself. Like your body, it works best when you are unaware of it.

But make your mind big, and you shall become big. Make your mind a world, and you shall encompass the whole thereof. No longer will you need to hide in the rubble of your sorrows!

"Yes," replied the sorrowful Tao Chien, "but tell me, how can a mind make itself great if all things are determined throughout all eternity—if the scroll is already fully written?"

And the wise one answered him, saying:

Man is a window between himself and the world beyond—and so, he sees all things through himself. But the window he does not see, for it is a part of the seeing. This do I call the great illusion, the necessary illusion, for all men act thereby.

Man is a window between himself and the world beyond. But many do not keep their windows clean. The world beyond looks hazy and formless—and so often do they see their own reflections in the dusty glass, that they believe the world beyond is also merely another distorted reflection.

I say unto you: not given entirely to any man is the *making* of his destiny, but upon his shoulders does rest its proper *fulfilling*. And only by perfection of self can one properly fulfill his destiny. Above all beliefs is this —a belief in one's own self!

Truly, the scroll is written, and not one word can be changed thereon. But the writing occurs day by day, and one does not always know what shall be written next. Therefore, the wise man unrolls it carefully, and his eyes are eager for the next line.

It is not the part he plays which determines the great man—but the manner in which he plays it.

And the true value of a man lies more in the greatness of his hopes than in the greatness of his accomplishments —for these latter frequently do not reflect his inner self.

No man knows the future—and the only man who shall have a future is he who believes he shall.

A man is no more than his thoughts. He who believes nothing, is nothing. And he who believes everything, is also nothing. For all things are known only by comparison. But he who believes in himself and his relation to the world about him—he is everything. For is not each a universe within and of himself?

This is the great misfortune of many men, that they have believing minds—believing in everyone and everything except themselves.

Yet a man's acts are guided less by what he is than by what he thinks he is. And he who has a poor opinion of himself can only act in a like fashion.

How can one assist another if he has no faith in his own strength?

There never was a great man who did not sense his own greatness—nor shall there ever be. For a part of the greatness, a vital part, lies in the realization thereof.

O my son! Believe in yourself. You are a child of the universe. Look forward to what was meant for you. Do your utmost in fulfilling your part in the vast and eternal scheme of things.

Man is a mirror in which nature admires herself. Let us see that the image is good, else she will be ashamed.

There is pride in the eyes of your mother, the earth. She expects much of you. And above all, she expects you to perfect yourself.

But many men believe that they do the acting, that they order all things—and this do I call the great illusion. In the smallness of their hearts, they are ungrateful. They are not proud of being a part of the universe, and its child; they want to control its every movement. They would be something separate and above.

Wash not the windows through which they look, else they may be blinded by the glare. And anyhow, with their childish ways, they have scrawled pretty pictures in the dust.

In a desert of trouble, how many a mirage has saved the weak of heart who otherwise would not have struggled on. Many a mirage has been a lake indeed.

The victory is worthless. The struggle makes the man. One reckons a goal by the distance which must be crossed thereto, and often an illusion makes a good goal.

But Tao Chien protested, saying: "Surely, this cannot

be! How can one reconcile truth with illusion?"[41]

And, as in answer to the paradox, a familiar voice spoke from behind his back: "Ah!—therein is your mistake! Is the material world in your brain? No, life itself depends on illusion."

Tao Chien turned to behold the speaker—but lo! *It was his shadow which had spoken!*

5

Lesson of the Stone

I heard the Accensus[42] proclaim the noon hour in the Forum, and stretched before me in all her luxury, lay Rome—capital of the earth!

Across the Forum, the great stairs of the palace lay muffled in the snow, and at Marmorata, "the haven by the river," the square blocks of white marble from the quarries of Luna were invisible in the whiteness.

For lo! Was it not the year 166, and the winter thereof? Even the marshes toward the sea—lately bright with dwarf-roses and wild lavender—lay like the vast white sands of the East!

Within the city, one could visit the drug shop of the famous Galen,[43] or the Vicus Tuscus with its incense stalls, shops of sandal-makers, and the flower markets where men hastened to and fro buying flowers to pin in the white folds of their togas—roses, the red and yellow winter roses of Carthage.

And I wondered that this should be so—that everyone was cloaked in holiday white, and that the aristocracy which lived on Mount Coelius lounged about the Forum, and that multi-colored banners floated from every height.

Then, from the direction of the Porta Triumphalis, my ears detected the distant call of triumpets, and still beyond these, the roll of heavy drums, the whistling of flutes, and the shouts of the people.

It was then I recognized the day—for it was the triumphal return of Marcus Aurelius[44] and Lucius Verus, co-emperors of Rome! They had come as victors after long and distant battles.

Slowly up the Via Sacra, toward the Forum, rolled the procession: trumpeters, elephants, white bulls for the sacrifice, wagons of glittering booty from the palace of Vologeses,[45] weary lines of clanking soldiers—and over everything, the white snow sifting down.

But in the midst of all the clamor, and in strange contrast thereto, appeared Marcus Aurelius—a calm face beneath a brow wreathed with laurel, a figure clad in gold-embroidered purple. Beside Lucius Verus, he stood in the foremost chariot, a huge chariot which was carved and gilded, and which was drawn by white horses. In his hand was a sceptre, but in his eyes only pity, and possibly—disdain.

And when darkness had fallen on the snow-covered streets, and the sacrifices to Jupiter Capitolinus were finished, and the sports at the Colosseum, and the banquets, Rome was again silent as the marshes upon which it rests.

And it came to pass that I beheld a group of torches that moved slowly toward the Temple of Peace,[46] and a weary figure in the midst thereof, clad in a simple toga, and I knew that it was Marcus the Emperor and philosopher.

Here were no Aetheopian slaves with skins of Falernian wine, here no merry-making, nor gold cages with chattering magpies—but only the quiet of empty lecture halls and a large library.

The tall braziers sent up a dim curl of smoke, and the firelight played upon the mirrors of beaten brass and the myrrhine vases, sending dull shafts of light across the room.

Above a table of old citron-wood, Marcus raised his torch and lighted a large three-wick lucerna which was hung against the wall, and which thereby waxed bright, scattering light upon the mosaics and the many rows of silver and carved ivory bosses at the ends of book-rollers.

And when the light had flickered into the corners of the room, he beheld an aged figure seated in the shadows at a distant table, and he saw that it was Fronto, which made his heart glad.

Thus spoke the aged Fronto:[47]

My Emperor and my son, I knew that you would seek the quiet of these halls after the noise of the mobs subsided. How fully has Rusticus[48] made you into a stoic! Look—you wear the toga of the street!

Perhaps you come to meditate on the victory that is never a victory, or the triumph that is never more than a name. Or, mayhap, you dwell on the causes of all these things.

But I, my Emperor, come to speak to you of these causes—if you will honor an old man with your ears. I have dragged these ancient warping legs over many roads to bring you my last lesson—the lesson of the stone. For I have grown old, and doom hangs as a cloud over Rome.

Many a man, as yourself, has had too sensitive a stomach to enjoy the butcher's job of war, and has turned in horror from the countless self-inflicted miseries of the masses. He would meditate with the stone and learn its lesson.

Thus philosophizes the stone: 'Why should I listen to the whispers of the wind and move? No movements I could make would influence my mother, the earth. I should only injure myself. But whenever she changes her shape and ways, then shall I move. And should I try to stop this movement, I should only injure myself.'

Thus philosophizes the stone: 'Lather yourself not with the froth of many doctrines. But be at peace with your mother, the earth. Observe her ways, and be wise. For he who moves against her, destroys himself.'

When you are at peace with the nature that gave you being, and developed your life, then, and only then, will you be at peace with yourself.

As for war, there can never be peace among men so long as there is not peace within the individual man.

War is merely the mass extension of the conflicts within the heart of the man on the street.

Those who are not at peace with themselves soon impose themselves on others. They search for something to blame for their misery, an outlet for their hatred.

But that man is at peace who guides his being and judges himself by the homely wisdom learned at the knee of his mother, the earth.[49] He has learned the lesson of the stone. He knows that changes in the nature of man means changes in nature as a whole.

All the laws of nature are laws of human nature—because, even to exist, they must be observed by man.

We speak loudly of nature—forgetting that we, too, are nature. And we speak even more loudly of the universe. Yet we are this also.

And just as there are causes for all things in the outer nature, so are there causes for all things in the inner nature —and these two are one and the same.

They that cry out against the causality that is all things, the drums that sound the roll of universal order and rhythm—theirs is the picture of a child which knows only its own room.

Speak not to me of luck and chance. It is only in a world of complete and rhythmic order that these are possible as fallacies of observation and excuses for ignorance. Forasmuch, if the world were partially or wholly chaotic, these would not stand out as exceptions.

Things are seen to exist only by comparison, and if the world were ruled by chance, then chance would not be recognized as such.

All things that move have causes and reasons sufficient to these ends. But not of themselves are these causes and reasons, but of the universe, its being, and its movement.[50]

The leaf that floats from the meanest tree—there is that which pulls it up, and that which pulls it down. But the tree says to itself: 'I shed the leaf, for I tired of it, and needed it no longer.'

The worm eats the tree, and the tree dons a cloak of pride, and says: 'Lo! Am I not kind? I have decided to house the lowly worm!' Yes, even when she is cut down, she thinks the fall to be solely her own doing.

All things are here because of the things before, and man cannot be reckoned unique among them.

The mind of man is like a deep stream reflecting the things that are, and the things that change. He knows the reflection to be within, and he proudly says to himself: 'I am a mover. I am a changer. And I *alone* have this ability.' He forgets the pebble which, by causing a landslide, moved as much earth in an hour as he had toiled to move in a century.

This do I teach—man is a movement, not a mover, and a causing, not a cause.

For the causes of all things, whether these be the thoughts of a man or the movements of a stone, are of the universe, by the universe, and peculiar to it.

And he that is in harmony with the universe is the happiest of men. Long are his days—and his nights untroubled. He has learned the lesson of the stone, and he moves not against the earth.

Let me speak of the values of this harmony, for he who is in conformity with his mother, the earth, cannot hate. Hatred and anger he can never know. He will always behold the cause and pity the source.

A blind dog falls into a hole. Does he growl at the hole? No—even the mind of the dog recognizes causes.

A strong wind blows a stick against you. Are you angry with the stick or the wind? Neither should you be angry with those who do evil unto you. Winds and sticks are they in forces which they do not see.

A strong wind blows a stick against you. A man does you evil. But wherein lies the evil? In the act? That is the stick. In the intention? That is the wind. No—the evil is within you, in that you saw it as such!

Merely because everything is according to nature, and a part thereof, does not mean that everything is good.[51] Neither does it mean that everything is bad. Whatever is, is neither right nor wrong, good nor bad. In and of itself, it simply is.

For behold! Good and evil are but shadows in your mind. Only the act has being—all adjectives attached thereto are yours and of you. And the act is that wherein the universe moves, but the good and evil are shadows thereof wherein the mind moves.

If one has done you evil, pity him that he is able to do evil—and look unto yourself that you may be done evil against!

No man commits an error or does evil thinking to have erred or done evil. Each thinks the act is right, and he has

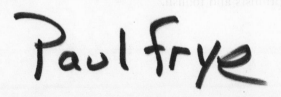

justified it to his own mind—else he would not have done it. Even the worst among us commit no mistakes purposely.

Men are not born criminals. Kind is the heart, and gay the spirit of one child even as another. But one grows to be twisted and distorted. He is made a criminal by society —the same society of which both you and I are a part.

The crimes of any one man are the crimes of all who have passed his way. And if he seeks shelter within your heart, and you close the door against him—who, then, is the greater criminal?

Greatest of all evils is this—not to be able to bear an evil. Herein lies the birth of fear and the urge for revenge.

Know, truly, that no evil is equal unto the fear thereof —or the anger it occasions.

If there were any reason to become angry, there would be just as much reason to remain so for all time.[52]

But all this is water over small pebbles and a wind among leaves. For an evil deed has evil as it is seen to be evil, and to another it may not be so.

Every man acts out of causes not wholly his own. When he does you wrong, view the causes—pity the mind that housed them.

He who sorrows because there are earthquakes and fires, is considered foolish. But how much more foolish is he who sorrows over the many lesser acts of nature which make men what they are.

Know in your own heart that evil is only a name. It is not the opposite of virtue—for weakness is the opposite of virtue, even as it is the opposite of vice.

Evil is only a name. There are those who apply it to all men and all acts. These are pessimists and foolish. There are those who apply it to no men and no acts. These are optimists and foolish.

But do not place yourself among those who cry out against evil, for he who hates evil hates mankind—and the hatred of a vice is in itself a vice.[53]

Have trust in your fellow men. What is seen is little. We must live by what we are told. Thus, our lives are held in trust by others.

Know that your value to mankind is no more than what you are worth to others.

And as for prophets, let it be known that every prophet of good is, by the same token, also a prophet of evil—for he is a drawer of lines. He who supposes a thing presupposes its opposite.

How foolish the rule—even as he who teaches it. For virtue cannot be taught any more than can genius. And codified morals and ethics no more produce moral people than do codes of aesthetics produce great artists.

In this world, we are as children. The mother does not stop the weeping of the child with moral sermons. On the contrary, she shows him that which is interesting in its beauty or its creativity. His attention to the bauble stems his flow of tears.

And I say unto you, you live in a world of baubles, beautiful baubles. Why, then, weep?

Weary yourself not with the word-worshipers who roll in their facile mouths the meaningless arguments of life, existence, and such. Take up that life, that existence, that universe. Behold it—beautiful is it, and a bauble beyond compare!

Why dwell *upon* life when you can live *in* life?

The causes of life itself, like all causes, are in the past—whereas I would tell you of the Now. He who grubs about the roots of a flower, loses its fragrance, and perhaps destroys the blossom itself.

Think not that evil is widespread in that it is much

spoken. Better known is the evil of one man, through gossip, than all the good of the city of his fellows through acclaim.

If evils were common, they would not be a subject for the gossip.

O my pity on those who seek out the evil, who find the shadow in every sunny day! For he who stares into the dark is blinded by the light.

The fig-leaf hanger says: 'We must cover its nudity with a leaf—lest it tempt the weak to evil thoughts.' Yes, nature to this small and empty heart was evil, and in the dry-rot of his own mind he ascribed this evil to the minds of others.

Where there is happiness and laughter, there is no need for moralizers, reformers, and their ilk.

Man's griefs would all but disappear were there not so many who find satisfaction in reminding him of them—for the recognition of grief is half the grief.

Dance, O my son! Let the rhythm of joy and the music of laughter set the pace! Away with these drab and dry drones, these despoilers of life, these hangers of crepe, and law-givers of the absurd!

Let this be known, that those who wish to lift up humanity must do so by natural means, and not by verbal artificialities. Man's basic structures cannot be altered by passing laws.

He who is so busy seeing that others are virtuous has little time to develop a virtue of self.

To him who would change the nature of man without resort to the methods of nature, I say—to so lift up man, one must get on a low level and beneath him!

Sin is the pang of a conscience squeezed by its own smallness.

He who recognizes evil recognizes enemy truths—and he who is an enemy to any part of the truth were better dead.

Know that an act is not evil which is not recognized as such, and it is not recognized as such by any save those who have an inner knowledge of it.

Actually, there is neither good nor evil except in obedience to natural laws—and these usually bring about their own rewards and punishments.

A deed of actual evil produces aversion in the many who know of it—and to this degree, it is a good.

All things actually evil ultimately destroy themselves.

O my son, would you get rid of evil? Behold! It is a word and a name—for who shall say what is evil?

We cannot say that one is evil merely because he commits an unworthy act. We can only say that his act is not in keeping with the ways of nature—and even this presupposes omniscience and is presumptuous.

We can only judge another as a silhouette in the light of our inner knowledge of him. And what a feeble light is such knowledge—even of our own parents!

Of him who speaks of the evil of others, I say: truly, he tells a drear tale of himself!

He who speaks evil of another probably will hear still greater evil spoken of himself. And he who slanders another actually slanders himself, and the other is praised by contrast.

In his judgment of others, one should never forget himself.

And of him who speaks of his own evil, I say: either he is the most honest of the honest, or the worst among the worse.

The herdsman calls the man a robber. The man calls the herdsman a murderer. But the cow stands calmly by and chews her cud. All three are right. All three are wrong. But the cow is wisest. She is silent.

When you would punish the criminal, beware—for the punishment might become worse than the crime. Who, then, is the criminal?

Lo! I give unto you a parable: A man had a fine herd of cattle, and this herd was strong and good. But there came, one day, another man who said unto him: 'Neighbor, you have a fine herd. All but a few have short horns. What a pity your herd should be ruined by a few long-horned cows. Long horns make for evil.'

And when the man had gone, the herder took aside his long-horned cows and slew them.

All was well, and he was satisfied until there came another man who said: 'Neighbor, you have a fine herd. All but a few are red. What a pity your herd should be ruined by a few black and white cows. Black and white make for evil.' And when the man had gone, the herder slew these also.

And there came still another man who found a part of the herd too slim—and these were slain. Later, under the same knife, went those cows which were too fat, and those which had short tails, and those with split teats—for all these things were evil.

And he became known throughout the country as a righteous man. But one day, there came a fellow herder who said unto him: 'Neighbor, what became of the fine herd you had but yesteryear?' And he answered: 'Alas! They all are slain, and better so—for all were evil.'

And so it came to pass that night departed from the Temple of Peace. And when the morning was come, Marcus and Fronto prepared to leave. But behold! Before the temple was a great red stain in the snow—like unto those seen in the Amphitheater after the games.

Marcus drew back and cried aloud: "It is an evil omen! An evil omen!"

From the lofty porticos of the Forum of Trajan, a dim vapour ascended into the skies, drawn by the sun from the morning snows. And over the marshes toward the sea, mists arose, poison mists—like the Lunar Virus, or the vapour that was loosed in the East.

Marcus beheld all these things, and he knew in his own heart that lean days had come to Rome, and that the days of happiness were no more.[54]

Thus it was that the great plague set in. People sickened at the touch, and all the priests of Aesculapius,[55] and all the wisdom of Galen, were to no avail.

There were not those of the living to bury the dead, and they lay on the streets, and among them was Cornelius Fronto!

6

Lament of Babylon

I, Nabonidus,[56] am of the blood of Babylon. Behold the works of my hands!

I have made sacred the houses of the gods, and raised the temple of the sun—and for the roof thereof brought five thousand beams of cedar from the northland.

For is this not mighty Babylon, with a hundred gates of brass, whose towers pillar up the heavens?

Broad and fertile are the plains whereon you lie at rest, O my Babylon.[57] You sleep between the breasts of Nisaba[58] on a soil as dark as the midnight woods of Ki.

How often have I stood between your palaces, on the bridge of stone and chain which spanned the river of your bosom![59]

How often have I climbed the tower, tier by tier, to the Temple of the Seven Spheres,[60] when the stars hung in the sky like sapphires, like gubba[61] stones from Sidon, and the night winds carried hints of cedar from the mountains of Sirara, or incense from the palace past the river!

Your star-towers were lofty, O my Babylon—like the obelisks of Egypt, like the Mountains of the Moon where the Aethiope is hiding, like the houses of the clouds beyond the river Indus![62]

Neither the houses of the clouds in that land beyond the Indus, nor the temples of that land, are so high as were your towers! The doves of Semiramus[63] fly not so high! Alas!—that you are fallen!

Alas! Your enemies have swept down upon you, as Sennacherib[64] of old—yes, even as the scorpion-men, and the monster, Lakhamu!

You have been filled with evil winds, your heart pierced, and your belly torn open as the belly of Tiamat.[65] Weep, O my eyes—for the world is rent asunder!

Give ear, O you Heavens, and hear the words of my mouth! I have wrought beauty, but it has been smitten under! I have sought after wisdom, but my tablets have they broken, and my towers thrown down!

O my Babylon! In the Hanging Gardens,[66] when the fountains tossed the moonlight on the walls of Lazuli, when the tinkling waters of the fountains were as voices of the zirri, were as fingers over harp strings—how often have I laid me down among your grasses!

Lovely were your Hanging Gardens, O my Mistress of the Valley!—like the almond trees that wave their silvery blossoms in the gardens of Sidon in the land of the Sidonites, like the golden galleys of Phoenicia, like the robes of the queens of Phoenicia!

Not in Phoenicia are there such gardens, nor in Sidon, nor in Tyre—the daughter of Sidon! Not in all the world are there gardens half so lovely! Alas!—that you are fallen!

Would that mine eyes had been plucked out by kites, and my heart delivered unto the dust, O my Babylon, that I might not have witnessed that which has come to pass!

For behold! The wild ass of the southern plains roams through the Hanging Gardens, over terraced grasses, under swinging censers in your alabaster arches!

From the vaults beneath the river, from the doors of either palace, swarms the poison-fly! Over your broken columns flap the wings of the wild bittern—and his cries bewail the hour, for the bones of your people lie unburied in the dens of mountain-wolves!

How can it be that you are fallen, O you who were born
of Ishtar, born of love, and were the axis of the whole
earth!

Your womb was plenteous with the riches of the world:
gold and silver, linen stuffs, ushu and ukarinu woods,[67]
uknu stones and beryls, yellow sea-clay,[68] apes, elephants,
birds of heaven with wings dyed purple, and chariots
from the enemy!

But now, your enemies have prevailed against you, and
they mock your shame. You have been shorn of your
riches, stripped of your jewels, and are naked before the
eyes of your slaves—even as Ishtar in the Land of No-Re-
turn! Yes, even as Ishtar beyond the seventh gate, they
have torn the last cloth from your loins![69]

O my Babylon, who are dead! You were born of love,
as is the son of man. You were born from a dream, as that
which issues from a jar hiding Siris, god of wines, like a
psalm on a flute of fire!

O my Babylon! How often have I lain in Ishtar's shrine
when the odors of sandalwood circled the Asherim, the
golden cones inlaid with pearl![70]

But all this is past, and gone, and a wind from the north.
Weep, O my eyes, for the winter of worlds. Beauty has
been slaughtered!

How often have I gazed at the great gate before Marduk[71]—with its thirteen rows of dragons, bulls, and uni-
corns, done in tilework blue and golden!

But all this is past, and gone, and a dreaming of dreams.
Weep, O my eyes, for the winter of worlds! Who again
shall sprinkle Ishtar?

On the altar which my hands had wrought, they have
set food of death before you—and these, your golden ves-
sels, flow with the waters of death.

Who shall fill the censers with sarbatu wood[72] and set a

flame thereto? Who shall recite the ritual to raise your fallen temples? There are none who know the tongue, and the tongue itself is stiff.

It was here, in Babylon, home of the beautiful, that the heavens were first mapped, and the laws of the universe first studied.

Truly, Babylon was proud. She built a tower to the heavens. She would examine the gods. But I say unto you —would there were more builders of towers, more examiners of gods!

Babylon was evil? But how could this be? Was she not both beautiful and wise? Where there is beauty, the word "evil" is a common complaint of the unsightly.

That which is beautiful has never brought forth evil— it has merely revealed the evil of others.

Without the rose, the thorn would go unnoticed; and the serpent would have been blessed had no one felt its venom.

O my friends, know that only that which is beautiful within can be beautiful without.

All evil having any basis in fact (and this is but a small portion of that commonly called evil) is derived from a common cause. It is disobedience to the natural laws of the earth—the laws permitting man's existence as an individual and a social animal, laws of the flesh, laws of the universe.

Let it be known that beauty does not thrive in a climate of actual evil. The body becomes palsied, wearied, old— even in youth. It bears the brand of evil, dissipation, grief —disobedience to the laws whereby the body itself exists.

To obey the laws of the universe, and your mother, the earth—and to be in harmony with these—such is to be beautiful and forever youthful.

And this is a commandment: create the beautiful. Anybody can create the pitiful and unsightly. He need only stay alive with a dead mind.

Create the beautiful, for the act of creation, and the urge thereto, is *love*—the order of the universe and its primary law!

He who creates has given himself over to an inner urge —to the pulsation of the universe speaking from within. He no longer stands lonely in his path. He is the mate of all that is universal and eternal, and he is pregnant with a child thereby.

Behold! The acts of love, the creations of the beautiful and wise, are everlasting. Civilizations come, and civilizations go, and all that remains of their past is the beauty they have created—the beauty of their arts and the beauty of the natural laws they have discovered. All men treasure these—the conquered and the conqueror.

Ring not too loudly this bell of civilization. Be not unduly proud. For all that is left of the civilizations of the past are their elements of beauty: their arts, and the truths they have discovered. Once-great names become but empty shells that echo these.

Art is living seed from the past. Look upon that which has gone before—some mouldy bones, some pictures carved in stone. These are the first records, and the bones were quickly buried.

Art is life in keeping, and all that is uniquely created or discovered is art. It requires an act of creation, and it is thereby a child of love. It becomes a mirroring of universal order, and a sounding-board for the eternal rhythm of all that is.

And I would apply this to *all* life, and I would declare that only he is happy who fulfills the urge for creation, who makes an art of his everyday life—and sees in that art the value of this life.

And just as the worthy art becomes eternal, so does the value of the life.

And let it be known that, of all arts, the art of living requires the greatest genius.

Be this a commandment: create the beautiful and unveil the true. The beautiful breeds the good, and it is the only climate wherein love can thrive—for who loves that which is distorted of body or mind?

But ever shall I cry out against those who give art a moral aim. Then will it cease to be art, done for the sake of the beauty it conveys, and it will be imposed as a duty. Messages should be sent by messengers. Art is the vehicle only of beauty.

And ever will my door be bolted against those who look upon art as an escape from reality, or the search for truth as an escape, or love. Thus will they devise confusion, disorder, unreality, and dislike—the child of disappointment.

One does not find beauty by turning his back on the world—for it is in this world, and of this world, and this alone, that all beauty has its being.

The beauty of a thing is sensed directly from its appearances. Though the hermit escapes into the wood to contemplate nature, the child who follows him need not contemplate. He feels the grandeur of the wood, senses the mystery of the twilight, and the beauty of the whole. To him, nature has spoken directly through its beauty.

It has been said that beauty is truth—and is it not so? Even as is the beautiful, so is the true that which is in conformity with the natural laws of the universe. How else could the beautiful and the true be identified or related?

It has been said that beauty and virtue and the 'good'

are all the same. And I declare that such is the nature of man, as a part of the universe, that he is virtuous when in conformity with its laws.

It has also been said that the beautiful is that which is pleasant—and verily, it is so. Only the urge for creation gives joy, whether this be the creation of a child or a work of art.

Know, O my brothers, that virtue, pleasure, truth, and beauty all have a common origin. They are a mirroring of universal order, harmony with universal rhythm. They are evidence, to be sensed by man himself, that he is in keeping with the ways of nature—the laws that led to his development.

That which is natural, however bad, is always more pleasant than the artificial. Thus, he who is worth much has no need for affectation in anything. Affectation is always the symbol of worthlessness.

Beauty is a robe of jewels and a mark of caste. It is a reward which the universe bestows upon the virtuous, the truthful, and the happy. All are rewards for obedience to her laws.

Behold! Upon your right, upon your left, the earth and the sky, and all that is contained between. Is not your mother, the earth, beautiful?

The earth is beautiful because it obeys the natural laws of the universe most closely. Even so, one may occasionally find a torn slope, a smouldering hill, a stricken tree.

So it is with man, for the human is the most complete development of order known to the universe, and the most intricate. Thereby, like the stricken tree, does he sometimes tangle in the web of causes—and thereby is he also sometimes unsightly.

And those who are unsightly are to be pitied and helped

—and never condemned. Pity those who have tangled in
the web of causes. Do you not, for the same reason, pity
those who are bearers of evil thoughts, and doers of evil
acts?

Because of the intricacy of man, it is inevitable that
there should sometimes occur a malformation in mind or
body. More often, however, one finds those who are
merely stunted in growth—the dwarf-men who are unable
to create. How great the pity that should be theirs!

And I say unto you—pity the small and deformed ones,
even as you pity the doers of evil. Let them not be a source
of your anger, even though they are acclaimed as 'wise'
men and betake upon themselves the rights of praise and
condemnation.

How can the non-creative know anything of the creative? Farther from each other than the farthest stars are
the creator and non-creator—the distance being that between gods and men. For truly, he who creates is a god.
Has this not always been the mark of a god?

And lo! Is it not strange that the men still judge the
gods, that the non-creative judge the creative? Still may
they be seen to sit, casting horoscopes, and expecting the
stars to obey!

Only he who is bewildered casts a horoscope for the
future. He cannot understand the present—and, perhaps,
he is afraid of what the past may have been.

O my friends, you have but one judge whose word is
final—yourselves. Your success and your happiness will lie
in *your* comparison between yourself and the universe,
and yourself and others. It cannot possibly lie in the comparison made by someone else, particularly someone who
cannot himself create. Be unto yourself, then, a judge.

In the hearts of all men, time will search out that art

which is to be eternal, and the critic and the non-creator will have no hand in this. For art which is only a sucking after fame, is rarely of value.

Only that art is of value which is a living of the present, and an expression of joy therein. Time, a process of the universe, will do the selecting.

What droll creatures inhabit the earth that there are those who sit in judgment on the course of the universe, and deem themselves wise!

And there is yet another secret I would make known unto you—that half the beauty of the world lies in the beholder.

What do we see in the beautiful that it pleases us? We see this—the awareness of beauty in ourselves that we may enjoy this music, this garden, this child, this picture—yes, this world about us.

Man is like unto a well, and some are deep, and others are shallow. Beauty is the reflection of love therein.

But lo! Many a well has crawling things on the bottom —and when the water is shallow, these are seen and magnified.

A string that is sounded makes a like sound in a like string—but what know the deaf of this? Thus it is they speak with their hands:

'This playing with strings—is it not childish? I can hear nothing, and what I cannot hear does not exist! How much better it would be to make money!'

The artist has always starved in the land of those who have only a belly—for few are the beautiful things which can be eaten!

How many an ass has made a supper of roses, and smelled none the better thereby!

Behold the non-creators! By their words may you know

them. They judge art by its defects—thereby revealing their own defects.

The flower that is torn apart, that it may be analyzed, emits no fragrance—nor do its scattered parts attract the wandering bee.

In this wise do the non-creators babble: 'It is sinful! It is a vanity! It cannot be used!' But who are the sinful, the vain, and the useless? Is it not they?

Art is creative and the child of love—even as the universe is creative and the author of love. Who would dare say that the universe is sinful, or vain, or useless—whatever this might mean?

Unto such as these, I say: Create the Hanging Gardens! Build a tower of Babel! Examine the gods! Map out the heavens! Then, and *only* then may you criticize Babylon!

7

In the House of Aspasia

This is a recording of events which took place following a festival of Apollo,[73] in the city of Athens, in the house of Aspasia,[74] a courtesan of Athens, in the eighty-fourth Olympiad:[75]

Behold the house of Aspasia, courtesan of Athens, beloved of Pericles the "long-head!" For the house of Aspasia was rich—yes, even in Athens, a city of riches!

On these walls lay the tapestries of Persia, wrested from Darius. Here sparkled the mosaics of Panenus,[76] brother of Phidias, and the wax works of many painters.

The hand of Callicrates cut the figures of the nymphs, sporting in their fountained caverns, and placed them in her halls—figures of jasper and spotted marbles, and the milk white stone of the Pentelic mountain.

Here, from jars about which curled the snakes of Bacchus,[77] flowed the wines of Lesbos and Chio—the red blood of grapes, the clear juice of figs.

For Aspasia, the courtesan, was wealthy—and she was beautiful. And like unto Thargelia,[78] she was also exceedingly wise.

From her lap, Pericles learned to control the city, and it was in her house that Phidias planned many of his works. Truly, she numbered among her visitors even Socrates, the wisest of men!

Here, to the ringing of cups, could be heard the laughter of youth, the mellow tones of Damon's lyre, or the burning poems of Sappho.[79]

Sophocles and Euripides found their critics in these rooms after the plays, and in these same rooms, Alcibiades wrapped his purple cloak around new and more beautiful women.

Tell me not that the silver sleuth-hounds of the Cyprian[80] no longer bay the hills of Greece—for so long as this house shall linger in the memories of man, so long shall the rose and myrtle grace the doorways of the heart!

And so it came to pass that, following a festival declared by Pericles, when the sun—Hyperion's[81] child—had trundled itself to sleep in the golden cup, and Dionysis[82] led a dance of stars in the sky, the radiant Aspasia entertained several of the best known men of Greece.

And thereamong were Empedocles,[83] Zeno, Phidias, and the young and effeminate Alcibiades.

Now Zeno and his visitor, Empedocles, came in want of a place to discuss philosophy. Phidias, ever in search of new ideas, came to listen. But the lisping voice of the youthful Alcibiades called only for drink.

Zeno and Empedocles seated themselves in a distant corner and took up their discussion. And here also came the lovely Aspasia, dressed in the scarlet silk of Cos, and laden with pearls.

She put her finger to her lips, and warned them, saying:

Athens is in religious turmoil, and even the slave is now being charged with heresy.[84]

No two thinking people, who are honest, can have the same religion or the same philosophy—much less the same god. Though Athens knows it not, these are matters of personality, and they will differ with individual personalities. Should the day ever come when it is recognized that these are matters of personality, and that no two can be the same, the world will be much more sane, honest, and far less bloody. But until then, we must guard our words!

Today, many a master is the slave of his slave!

At one time, all humanity cried: 'He is a sorcerer! He is a sorcerer! Burn him!'—and he perished in the flames.

A few centuries later, one lone man said: 'I found a sorcerer, and I slew him.' And all humanity cried: 'He is a murderer! He is a murderer! Burn him!'—and he also perished in the flames.

Such is the difference of a few years. It has happened in the past, in one way or another, and it will doubtlessly happen again and again.

The originality of today is the lethargy of tomorrow.

When all accept an opinion, everyone ceases to think about it—whether it be good or bad, harsh or helpful, tyrannical or free. It only remains to dispose of the dissenter.

When an individual opinion is destroyed, there die the opinions of all men.

The dissenter is the gad-fly of thought—for opinion universally accepted is thought paralyzed.

Know, O Empedocles, that as soon as all men accept a given principle, the principle frequently is made both harmful and fallacious—harmful because it prevents further original thought on the issue, and fallacious because no two people are the same, and neither are any two situations.

All truth, save the natural laws of the universe, is untruth, or—at best—only partial truth.

Men are basically unequal, and save for their sensing of the influence of universal laws, they have no common opinion of their own.

Athens is in a sorry condition. The customs, once devised to help men understand each other, now have been fashioned into the chains of law. Therefore, that which was once worn as a bracelet in adornment is now worn as a shackle in subjection.

When it is required of a man that he do thus and so, then he does thus and so. But his heart is not in it. Of such is the nation whose customs have frozen into laws. The body obeys. The mind rebels. And the heart is sick—for it is a nation controlled by fear.

There is a difference between a request and a demand, between an expectation and an order—and the difference is the self-respect and pride of the man to whom the order is given.

He who acts by custom does so that he may not be misunderstood or misjudged, and the act is his own—the act of a free man. But he who does the act because it is demanded by the law, acts either out of blind habit, or out of fear. And if he thinks about it, there may be hatred in his eyes.

The culture whose customs are largely laws, is no longer a culture.

Many a man would do what is necessary were it not demanded that he do so.

Man, to exist, must be a social animal. And society, to exist, must follow certain social and moral laws. These are merely social extensions of the individual law of self-preservation, and they are ultimately necessary for the lives of the individual members of the society. Such laws, morals,

rules, or customs are common to all societies and all re-
ligions. They are not god-given, but rather, were evolved
out of social necessity, and by mutual agreement, after
much conflict and chaos. Therefore, the complete freedom
of man, as a social animal, is unobtainable. It is a false
ideal.

And let this be known—that if all men were equal, laws
would be unnecessary. But since no two men are equal,
the very existence of humanity depends on the laws of
society.

And it should also be realized that in man's basic in-
equalities, lies the inherent injustice of all laws—for that
which is just for one must be unjust for another.

If all men were wise, justice could be dealt to a man as
an individual, and not as a transgressor of some blanket
law.

But this is idle chatter—for if all men were wise, it is
doubtful whether laws would be needed. Wise men are as
rare as equal men.

O my friends! I would tell you of the unequal. Of the
equal, I cannot speak. Enough of this mouth-froth! How
can one speak of that which does not exist?

In all this universe, there are no two things that are
equal, and no two races, and no two communities, and
no two men of any race or community.

It is the nature of all things to be unequal. Two things
that are equal are the same thing.

Only with inequality do you find the movement that is
life. If there were no high, and there were no low, and
neither an up nor down, how would the rivers run—and
where would he seek who sought after the heights?

You who ride the winds in search of new heavens—is not
your search an up-going, a longing for greater inequality?

What need to fly if all were equal? Then, indeed, might you clip the wings of thought.

Only in death is there equality. But in your differences is your life, and in your differences also your hope—so speaks the universe.

On! I cry—and up! The inequality of men is their common good. In this lies their salvation!

There is little difference between men—but in that little lies their value.

And in one sense, one kind of equality within the whole of society, is based upon the inequality of its members. For example, a body of extreme individualists—when observed as a whole—must necessarily represent an extreme socialization. Otherwise all the separate members could not be complete individualists.

O my friends! Only one equality would I strive for—the equal opportunity to be unequal!

But thus has it been said, and often: 'All men are born free and equal.' And yet have I to see two that are equal, or even one that is free.

And what is this freedom which men worship? Is not worship itself contrary to freedom—is there not a neck-noose even in this?

So shall you always find it—that the strongest of all shackles are words!

And what shall it profit a man to lose his ankle chains if his mind be in a cage? Alas! Too many, far too many such are loosed upon us.

Many a man has broken his ankle-chains and thrown them down in the path. And those who have followed him have stumbled thereon, and fallen.

This do I believe, that most often a man has but one prisoner—himself!

However, slaves there are—and plenty of them—in our societies. You may call them what you will: serfs, bondsmen, laborers, slaves, peasants, or workmen. It is only a matter of degree, and a mouthing of different names.

Any man who has not, for his own thoughts and his own pleasures, a half of his every day, and the life with which he was born, is thereby a slave—whatever other names he may be called.

A slave can be defined in no other way than this—he is only a man who finds little pleasure, and therefore little of his own life, in the days his mother, the earth, has given him.

Great as is the drawer of water and the hewer of wood, culture owes less to these than to the leisurely!

The pitiful self-slavery of man! He dwells in anachronism. Long does he toil, and wearily—because his heart is fond of leisure!

One must pay out entirely too much of his life to his fellow men merely for the right to live! It is truly a pitiful condition of mankind. For it is the earth, his mother, whom he owes for his life—and his fellow men are exploiting him without cause.

Labor is not a virtue. Its sole objective is its own abolition—for only those products of labor are good which improve leisure and make labor itself less necessary.

Labor is a vice. Play is a virtue. Yet they may both be the same man at the same wheel! And how shall we know the labor from the hard play of the healthy? Look for the smile. Listen for the laughter!

It is the freedom of the act, and the joy of the acting, that defines the act as play. Many a drawer of water and hewer of wood would refuse to have it otherwise. Yes, many such have played throughout their lives and have not known the meaning of work.

But not a few such have spent all their lives shouting for freedom—and thereby denouncing themselves.

And there are also those who betray their longing for self-escape by shouting against freedom. But these are only the ones who have realized their own self-enslavement and have learned to feel lonely therein.

Has not many a moth, caught in its own cocoon, learned to hate the wind and light—and ended life by gnawing off its own wings?

All true freedom must come from within. For the most part, it is an attitude and an outlook. It can only be judged in relation to one's hopes, ambitions, and desires!

And most of those who feel enslaved are merely obsessed by foolish or impossible ambitions.

Few men, today, are owned by others—but even fewer own themselves!

Man is a creature of two legs. He is supposed to stand erect! And I can forgive him whose legs are stiff—but why is it we have the kneeler and the crawler?

As a child, man is a crawler. But even when the body has long walked, in how many a man does the spirit still crawl!

In this world of ours grow many trees of crutches—crutches for the legs, but mostly crutches for the mind. Each tends his own tree, else the father would soon crawl with the child.

Let it be known, then, that most people who cry out for freedom wish to be freed from things with which they have concerned themselves—but not the things which have concerned them.

True freedom lies in servitude—servitude to oneself. It is self-realization and fulfilment of being, and not mere rights of self-assertion.

He who wishes to be a hewer of wood, and who must

be a monarch—he is his own slave, and also a failure. And he who is capable only of hewing wood, but mourns that he is not a monarch—he is his own slave, and also a man of foolish and false ambitions.

Only he has made a success of life, and has found freedom, who is what he wishes to be and does what he wants to do—or, conversely, he who has adjusted his wants and wishes to what he is and does.

The slave has no pride of self—and little personal honor. But the man who is free is both a proud man and a man of honor.

Blessed in my eyes is the proud man. In him personal honor takes the place of cowardice. As a cliff against the storm, he stands strong in his own path!

Show me that workman of whom it can be said: 'He takes joy in his work, and does it well—but he has no pride in it.'

Without pride, there is no ambition. And the highest ambition is that of the most proud—self-perfection.

When one has ceased to be proud of his life, his friends should look proudly upon his death—and he should see to it that this may be so!

So spoke Aspasia, the beautiful, as she looked at those about her. And in her eyes was the pride of which she spoke—but not the love which would so well have accompanied her beauty.

But in the heart of Empedocles, there was only darkness —for her words brought down the temples of his dreams, and in his ambitions he now saw only false hopes.

Whereupon, Empedocles arose. And he made no answer, but left the house, and left Hellas, and was seen no more.

And there are those who say that he was swept into the sky, and there are those who say that he was breathed into a great mountain of fire.[85] But only this is known for sure, that before his passing, he had said:

"Oh my friends—unto you now do I walk as god, no more as man!"

But this was later, much later—and none knew what was meant thereby, and the story had become confused.

8

The Unwritten Sura of Mohammed

It was Abulquasim, the reformer—*Abulquasim ben Abdallah ben Abdelmottalib el Hashimi,* and he called himself Mohammed, meaning the "glorified," the prophet of Allah. But cycle follows cycle, and of all prophets only the prophecies remain.

And so it came to pass that a sickness descended upon Mohammed, and during a darkness of the mind, he visited a graveyard where he congratulated the dead on having found peace.

Thursday, the eighth Rabi el Awwal, the sickness became worse, and the ending had begun. It was then Mohammed cried: "Hasten! Bring me writing materials that I may write down what is to be remembered after me!"[86]

But dissension broke out among his disciples, and Omar the Conqueror, who became Caliph after Abu Bekr, said: "Pain is deceiving the prophet! We have the Koran—which is enough!"[87]

And the last words remained unspoken. The last Sura, the dying revelation, remained unwritten. And so it was when Azrael,[88] who was Death, came into the room.

And lo! The form of Azrael was that of Khadija,[89] Queen of the Caravans, his first love.

Like the cool evening winds from the east, she drew in the curtains and entered. Her silks were the green of Khaiber grass, and her veil a star-mist behind which flashed the dark and thunderous eyes of Azrael. And thus, she laid the cold of her hand upon his brow, and said:

O Mohammed! O world-departing one! Raise your head from the lap of Aisha.[90] For it is in your own behalf that these words are given, and it would do you well to listen thereto.

From distances of many marching days have I ridden the winged horse, Boraq,[91] that I might find you and speak with you while you are yet in human form.

From the shade of the Lote Tree on the right of the throne,[92] over ten-thousand times ten-thousand seas of rainbow light and deepest shadow, through floating clouds of hyacinths, gauze, and fire, have I come to you.

And the hoofs of Boraq rang like midnight bells on the silver soil of the garden of paradise. We flew the mountains of amber and scattered the gravel of pearls in the valleys.

For I carry the seal of Azrael, Keeper of the Books, Commander of the hundred-thousand legions of Death—and I carry also a warning, O self-appointed one—long and bitter has been the weeping for your deeds!

O Abulquasim—yes, let me call you Abulquasim,[93] for thus did I know you. But I know you no more. How you have changed since last you hid yourself in my skirts!

When the sands whispered with the voices of Djinns,[94] you came to me, and I comforted you. When you were treated as a liar, I believed in you. When you were poor, I enriched you—and appointed you master of my caravans.

And we were married. At the feet of the idol, Hobal, I drew the dart which made us one.[95] A camel was slain and divided among the poor. Many a skin of date wine flowed, and the slave girls swayed to the music of the tambourines and timbrels beneath the shifting light of the torches.

You were kind and gentle, my Abulquasim, and they called you *el amin,* the trustworthy, the sincere. You sheltered the weak, and you gave unto those who had nothing.

Yes, when the Kaaba[96] was rebuilt with timbers from Jeddah, it was you they chose to place the stone therein!

But all this was long ago, and before you grew powerful. Fame, and wealth, and power—these are the things which have twisted you until your heart is as dry as the nofuds, the reaches of bloody sands, and your thoughts like a wild dwarf palm.

What of the *ahl es suffa,* the people of the bench?[97] They stole camels, and you cut off their hands and feet, and pierced their eyes, and left them by themselves on the sands—where they died. Yet, have you not also stolen camels?

O you who were conjured up out of sorry-water and reared in triple darkness! You have betrayed your trust, slain your people, and stolen the wife of your own son![98] You have been treacherous and cruel.

This do I say—better were the world in idolatry than under your standard, for the idol cannot wield the sword that slays, the idol cannot take itself to treachery and lies!

The Banyu Qayla[99] were satisfied with their wooden statue before you rode into Yathrib on your camel. And the pilgrims made their seven rounds of the Kaaba in all contentment before you returned. And these trips had a meaning—for they were a symbol of the motion of the lordly stars, and the rhythm of the universe.[100]

O Abulquasim! As you loved me, believe this: Allah is

merely the universe, and nothing more. Listen and learn, for I come from beyond the Lote Tree on the right of the throne.

Can you not recall? You were told this by your townsman, Nadhr ben el Harith, who had journeyed into Iran. But you would not believe.[101]

He brought you tales of Iran, and the story of the universe, and the sun, and the glory of the whole. But you would not believe. And years later, you had him chained —and you slew him!

But Nadhr ben el Harith has won! Even in death has he won—for he spoke the truth. Allah is the universe, as would be any other god, for there is nothing other than this. And the universe has no prophets, O my self-styled prophet!

The universe cares naught for your Kaaba, nor the stone therein. It cares naught for your chants, nor your razzias.[102] And it gives no laws save those of its own eternal order and rhythm.

Close your eyes that you may see. Stop your ears that you may hear. You cannot know earth, if you have not known heaven—so far is earth above your heaven!

Weak are they, and a part of the many, who do not build into the skies—but foolish are those who build, but fail to lay their first stones on the soil!

O my Abulquasim! How you have deceived others in deceiving yourself! Truly, you built into the skies—but all was a vision and a vapour of the mind. Your feet are dark with the blood in which you walked, and the earth knew not that your hand had built!

It is indeed pitiful that most of those who are well-known to others, know little of themselves!

Yours was the ambition of the most vain—for you played

upon the superstitions and hopes of those about you in order to achieve power and fame.

Of all the characteristics of the human, the urge for power is the most selfish, the most immoral, the most vicious, and the most indicative of the primitive wolf which still prowls the inner recesses of his being.

Born of fear and a sense of inferiority, the urge for power is basically a quest for security. But it too frequently twists a man into the paths of vengeance. He thereby proves his inferiority and elaborates his fears.

Only that individual who has misdirected his own life seeks to direct the lives of others.

Why should anyone desire power over another unless he has failed to realize power within himself?

Out of this darkness of the heart come the war-mongers, despots, and reformers such as yourself, my Abulquasim.

Given to no one is the right to dominate the life of another, and when that right is usurped, you have slain him as an individual. You are his social murderer.

Therefore, he who is intent upon reforming humanity, had best start by reforming himself—for in that intent lies the greatest possible need for reformation.

Of all virtues, tolerance is the only one absolutely necessary for the existence of society—and of all people, the reformer is least tolerant. In truth, he is avowedly intolerant, and seeks to make a virtue of it.

Ambition may be directed into many channels. But the desire to shape the lives of others is the worst among them.

Of ambition we need not speak. They that have it cannot stop. And they that have it not, cannot start.

And the greatest of all ambitions is self-perfection. And the most foolish of all ambitions is fame—a turning away from the self, a deserting of the present for the future.

He who seeks after power, fame, or wealth—the goals of self-aggrandizement—does so at the expense of his fellows. And his happiness is frequently the misery of many. But he who seeks after self-perfection benefits both himself and those about him.

True fame and power exist in respect and admiration, and the more obviously these latter are pursued, the less likely they are to be attained. One does not admire him who seeks admiration as a value in itself.

And even of him who has obtained fame, let it be known that he shall live in brass—yes, and turn green with the passing of time.

No commodity is worth less, nor is more perishable than fame.

And be sure of this—the greater the merit of a man, the less chance of his recognition, save by the very few. And as for the genius, he is always left to mould a hundred years.

Only that which is familiar can be recognized—and there are indeed few who are familiar with the lofty ideals or rare accomplishments of others. Therefore, these others usually find themselves as strangers in a world knowing the whip-hand of power and wealth.

For this reason, at the table of fame there are always empty chairs for rich stupids and successful butchers of the human race—but the genius eats on the stones outside.

O my Abulquasim! He who strives after fame lives in the non-existent tomorrow, and gives away his present.

Most often, fame is merely the words wherewith people flatter him whom they cannot understand. It fills their bellies. It is wines to their tongues. For by this means do they raise themselves as his judges.

You who are in search of fame—are you, then, so sick

of your freedom that you would have no moment for your own? Do you, then, prefer that your private life be turned to public use?

A slave is no less a slave merely because of many masters.

He who serves another serves up himself—and the heart that graces a platter cannot beat in a breast.

Know that he who accepts the plaudits of the public must share in the responsibility for that public. And this is his only reward—that he is subject to their ever-changing and unthinking whims, and is alternately condemned and praised. They are as children, and when his usefulness to them is past, or when they find a brighter bauble, he is forgotten. And should his private life, or deeds, or opinions, run contrary to these whims at any time, he is speedily punished—and possibly slain.

Let this be your warning—that every truly great man who has become famous, and has tasted of the cup, has rejected it, disliked it, and denied it whenever possible. And the wiser of these have sought long and hard to avoid it.

Fame, in most lands, can be purchased—and even this is sufficient to condemn it.

O my friend! Look about yourself, and ask: 'Are these strangers the judges of my value to humanity? Have they shared in these matters more than myself, that they pass judgment?'

Only the fame that exists as a voluntary repayment of active love for one's fellow men can endure. All else is passing fancy, and soon gone. It must come as a natural appraisal and appreciation of one's benefactions to humanity.

Doubly great is he whose greatness is within himself,

yet displaying it not, he is judged great by others.

When has the wise man become the wiser for being recognized?

Realize that he who is praised by those who do not understand him, is being flattered. Many cannot understand the truly great man, or the genius. Hence, his fame is often no more than the flattery of the many.

When great men behold their critics, then do they discover that the first evidence of true greatness is to be unknown.

Two ways do the unknowing deal with the truly great man, the genius, or anything else they do not understand: either they flatter, and thereby raise themselves as judges —or they condemn, thereby also raising themselves as judges. In either case, it is a breath in a summer wind, and a way they have of praising themselves.

But most often, he who is observed to excel becomes an outcast—for he arouses the envy of those about him.

Further, there is nothing more resented by the many, than *change*—the very thing which gives them their existence. And he who excels in any fashion, represents change.

If ever you feel that fame is more than words of waste, look upon the bones of wise men who have either starved or burned—and look also upon the military butchers, begowned stupids, fame-rabble, and the word-worshipers.

And behold the ends of these latter ones—for the highest tree is that which is first struck by lightning. And it is this tree, easily seen, which is first felled by the woodsman.

Thus runs the logic of the fame-rabble: 'They say he is great—therefore, he is great. It has been written!' But the next one may read from a different book.

Fame is merely being heard of by those of whom one

has not heard, nor cares to hear.

How can honors be conferred on anyone? Like unto ambition, one either has honor, or he has it not. And he who has honor values it, nor will he accept it as charity due to a passing whim of the public.

Know, also, that 'honors' given by those without honor, are in themselves dishonorable.

Further, the 'honors' heaped upon a person, bring responsibilities, and are evidence that society is ready to domesticate his originality, classify him, and bring him into the social pattern.

Yes, fame is frequently only flattery, and just as often false as true. And for every one who speaks such flattery, there are a thousand to listen.

O my Abulquasim! In your search for the man you wanted tomorrow, the *afterman,* you have lost the present man. And you leave nothing for the earth but your body!

And lo! Mohammed—he that forsook the present for the future, beheld the future! Before his eyes, the heavens folded, and the mountains became as carded wool driven before the wind! Khadija was gone—and before him stood the *afterman!*

Mohammed groaned and hid his face in the skirts of Aisha. And the prophet-that-is gazed down at the prophet-that-was!

Mohammed was dead. And those that remembered him died, and those that remembered them. Only the afterman lived, as the prophet-that-is—intricacies of vapour, mosaics of words, words, words. Down, word-worshipers! Behold the afterman!

9

Worshipers of Mammon

On the sea I was nine uinals[103] and seven kins to the south and west, with the evenings hot, and a good wind.

And on the seventh kin, which was the Day of the Deer, in the Month of the Fruit-fall, I came to a land of tall mountains. The valleys thereof were surpassing rich with wild fig trees wherein the spider-monkey swung. Green was the earth, and the air sweet with the scent of wild vanilla. There we put into a small lagoon, which was fed by a mountain stream.

And wherever I turned my eyes, I saw at a distance the cities and temples of the Ancients—now almost asleep beneath the curtained green of the forests.

And when I came upon them, lo! All was emptiness and silence! Only the drone of insects broke the slumber of centuries. The stones of the temple courts were thrust up where grew the great sapota with its apples,[104] and no pillar stood thereon but was wreathed with the tear-vine.

The palace walls, which bore the carvings of the kings, were rent asunder by the hands of time—and in the crevices made thereby, was stored the honey of the stingless bee.

Here, amidst the ruins of the past, I dwelt until the five nameless days were come[105]—at which time I followed Kinich Kakmo (who is the sun) into the west.

And thus, it came to pass that, after a day's journey by

foot, I heard in the air a making of music—which I knew to be the singing-winds. And before me stood a mighty monolith of jade, carved with figures strange and moving, as though in warning to him who travels here. But, beyond, lay the path of the Ancients leading into the Garden of the Heart! Yes, the Garden of the Heart, rubbed from the codex by some doubting scribe of aeons gone![106]

High among mountains like green stalagmites, a cloud-mist hides a valley of many shadows wherein lies the garden, and the earth watches over it closely.

Here flows the river of yesterday, into a broad lagoon, but the water is never gone, and the lake is never filled. And here blows the wind of yesterday—but never a tree has lost its leaves.

Deep is the valley, and narrow. The shade of a crow, passing above, bends its pinions on the walls. It flutters, as a ghost, between the stones. The stones are unreal to the realm of the shade, but it dies among them. Like unto the life of man is the shadow of this crow!

Deep is the valley of many shadows. And at sunset, one lone ray of light stabs the heart of the stream below, leaving a bloody trail. It makes no gap, no wound in the stream—yet the trail of blood is there. Like unto the heart of man is the heart of this stream!

But soon the stream flows into a broad lake, and there the valley had allowed itself to widen. And there it was, on the western shore, that my eyes beheld a great avenue leading through a garden surrounded by wild lime trees. And lo! Above them, and in the midst thereof, a temple proudly reared its terraced slopes!

Beautiful, from the mountains, was the temple in the Garden of the Heart—beautiful beyond the mortal sight; and I saw that it was built of obsidian, inlaid with crystal, wherefrom the sun struck out a multitude of colored lights.

Here lay the Garden of the Heart, past the great stelae of the Ancients. And when the huge censers in the temple have been lighted, here one dons his sandals for his evening walk between the rows of blossoming limes. In the heavens, the sunset strikes the feathers of the Quetzal bird with green and gold,[107] and the winds mix the aroma of pom-incense[108] with the dusky scent of wild vanilla.

So I dreamed—for ages long ago was built the Garden of the Heart, in a day when the moan-bird[109] did not cry, and men were not blind as Zotz, the bat.[110]

It was then that Votan, born of the House of Chan, the Serpent, was made high priest of the temple—or so the legend runs.[111] Upon returning from his long journey to the land of the terraced towers, the land of Valum Chivim,[112] he talked with the Sowers of Flowers, the men of the curved mountain, and those that dwelt on the floating gardens of the west.[113] He then turned his eyes toward the valley of many shadows—where he founded the city of Nachan and laid out the Garden of the Heart.

All these things passed through my mind, as a haze of legend and history, and I ran the length of the valley toward the garden. But lo! When I arrived and looked about me, I sickened, and turned away my face!

It was spring, but there were no flowers, and the thistle reared its horns in gardens where no bird sang. Earth was bare, forsaken—and I laid me down and wept at desolation made so manifest.

Yes, I ran my fingers through the soil and wept aloud with tears of youth—crying vengeance on him who had strewn salt in the Garden of the Heart.

Then, from the rubble of the temple above, I heard a cry like that of a stricken eagle, and an old and faltering voice which asked:

What are you doing here, Stranger, in the Garden of

the Heart? Look upon the weeds, the darnel and the tare
—for all paths are closed!

Even upon the stone is gathered the hoar-frost of salt.
It is the Age of Tears, and tears were ever salty.

Have you not heard—Honor has been dead these many
years, and Virtue has departed. Behold! Mammon rules
supreme.[114] I, Votan, was the first, and now am the last!

Thus, it came to pass that I questioned him not, but
turned my face north from the Garden of the Heart, and
left by the path that few have trodden since. For I was
sick within, and filled with a loathing for whom or what
I did not know.

Many uinals I traveled until, at last, my eyes were made
glad with the tall spires of a mighty city—the tallest in the
world.[115] Like unto silver crystals they stood, beautiful
beyond comprehension!

"Surely," I said to myself, "this must be a city of great
learning wherein dwell only the wise and the deep of
heart—for are these not star-towers?"

But lo! What I did not see was the use of the city, and
the way of its life—for its beauty was that of a harlot in
the market, and the signs of its dissipation and decay
were seen in the festering sores of its slums!

The buildings, which I had thought to be star-towers
for the study of the heavens, were only the temples of
money-changers, for the city was suffering from a sickness
within. About me were the slime trails where coin had
rolled—and few are those who can stand upright in such
a slime!

And in the midst of the city I beheld a huge and hideous
idol, whereon was inscribed with letters of gold: DOWN,
SLAVES! THIS IS MAMMON!

And I looked about for Virtue, and I found her on a corner in the market—and the unwashed played in her skirts and made sport of her!

And it was told me that everything has its price today, but cheapest of all is Virtue. She is a prostitute in the temple of Mammon.

Everything has a price today, but few are the things that have a value.

Too often the virgin is found only in the womb of her mother—for she is but the idle dream of love-sick youth. Flesh has no value under Mammon.

And I went in search of Honor, but found only his sister, Hope, weeping over the grave. And here, too, were weeds and the neglect of years.

And I asked those who stood in a forward place: "Where is love?" But they looked bewildered, and answered: "We know her not."

Whereupon spoke an ancient woman: "There was one here who called herself Love. But that was many years ago. She sickened and soon left."

Then did I grow angry—as never before nor since—and I turned unto them, crying:

Wretches! You have sacrificed everything of true value to your idol, Mammon!

Behold the great among you in this place of crawling things—they were turned out of the Garden of the Heart, being thieves, and liars, and murderers!

This have I to say of the gold you worship—it has a few worthwhile uses. But the making of money is not one of them!

The only gold of true value lies in the sunlight, and he who loses this is poor indeed.

O you pitiful ones! You have broken up your sun to coin your god. Now must you carry on your business in the dark. But, mayhap, it is better thus—for such business belongs to the dark.

Who was that fool who thought to have rid us of the golden calf? Blind was he, and in need of eyes! Has not the calf become a bull—else whence came these many who are gored?

This shall I ever cry out, O you coin-rabble: that the gathering of gold is not a sign of superiority—unless the thief be superior!

A thief is a thief—whether he does his stealing legally, as a money-changer, or seizes it by force.

The money-changer is only a thief who is also a coward. He hides behind the law and preys upon the poor, the honest, and the trusting. He is a priest in the temple of Mammon.

And thus does he shout: 'You should not fight back, for that is illegal—and the laws are sacred!'

But to his fellow priest, he adds the whisper: 'If we cannot wax rich enough by these laws, we shall make new ones!'

But I say unto you: they that make money from money, without creating anything, are parasites and leeches. They suck blood from their fellow men!

O you worshipers of Mammon! Is this, then, your highest ideal, your greatest goal—to be a sucker of blood, a leech?

Know that he who has money has power. But power should be only in the hands of the intelligent, the honest, and the meritorious. And if only these obtained wealth, I too would worship in the temple of Mammon.

He that has money has power. But the getting of money requires only *shrewdness*—or, perhaps, the chance of birth, or unscrupulousness. And the greater part of all wealth has these origins. Yet these are not intelligence, and neither are they virtue. Herein dwells the greatest living lie of our times!

And upon this lie is based still another lie. Thus, in his heart, the money-changer says: 'Price and value are the same—except when I am cheated.'

But the genius starves in the street, while the legal thief and the shrewd fool live in plenty.

And where are those who would beautify the world—the artist, the poet, and the musician? Go! Ask the gutter rats!

If you are in search of bitter men, men who have turned against the world, whose hearts are warped, whose spirits dried, look at those who have sought after the truth—only to find that it had no value among the swine who snout the soil for Mammon.

For thus speaks the Mammonite: 'The meaning and existence of all things lie in their usefulness, and their price is the same as their value. Thereby shall we judge and test them.'

But have you not noticed that the usefulness or uselessness of things is most often directed by the whims of each worshiper, and that in no two is it the same?

And how shall we fix a price on the sunlight, or the morning shower—and what money-changer has set up a bargain counter to deal in the winds wherewith we breathe? And yet, are these not the most useful of all things?

Have you not noticed that, under the rule of Mammon, he is rewarded the least who does the most for humanity? The coat of the teacher is threadbare in order that the great military butcher may wear his gold-braid!

What or where are morals or values in a society which

gives its highest rewards for selfishness, greed, and legal thievery—and its honor to those who have money, though they have nothing else?

Behold! Dishonesty is a shield today—for he who trusts his brother bares his throat for the knife!

Truly, only the plant need no longer blush for the seeds it bears!

Blessed are the blind today, that they cannot see. For the death agonies of Honor are not pleasant to the eye.

Blessed are the deaf, that they cannot hear. For the ears are torn by the screams of Virtue where she lies stripped and assaulted by the unwashed.

Many men hurry about the city today. There is to be a sacrifice. But lo! Can this tortured and disheveled creature, bound on the altar of Mammon, be the once proud and beautiful Virtue—can this be she?

O you worshipers of Mammon! What do you hope to gain with wealth?—peace? But it is not for sale. Show me that market wherein peace is sold!

Peace comes with trust. There can be no peace among the worshipers of Mammon. Each must keep guard against his own brother.

And he who gains the most wealth is thereby assailed the most—and it is he who must keep the closest guard, and has the least peace.

If you wish peace, then turn unto your mother, the earth—but money will not help you.

Perhaps, you think to buy love? But tell me not the price paid for a heart—any price is too high for carrion. You bought a heart? For what—food? The crows have refused it!

The woman who takes a man for money is a prostitute —even though she be a virgin. Instead of selling herself day by day, she has merely sold herself by contract.

Perhaps you hope to buy honor? But can honor be purchased? Is this not bribery?

You poor bewildered fools! There is not one worthwhile thing on the face of the earth which can be obtained with money!

Behold! You have made an end out of a means. Many of you sit, cold and wet, in the evening rains as the nighttime of life approaches. Why did you destroy the tent to carve an idol out of the tent-pole?

Have you yet seen a man leave this life taking with him his wealth? When a man of merit dies, the race grieves. But when a money-changer dies, humanity is both relieved of a parasite and profited by his wealth.

Only that is of value which is, by its attainment, a value to all. Such, for example, are happiness, social harmony, self-perfection, and physical well-being.

Thus, one should never gather unto himself that which cannot become a part of himself.

Money is of value only as a means of bettering humanity. But it is used chiefly to obtain more money—and no other end is seen.

And this is usually the great sorrow of the wealthy—that they never live long enough to learn how to use that which they have gathered!

'Tomorrow,' they say, 'we shall live at ease, and perfect ourselves—and we shall also assist others to live at ease and perfect themselves.' But only the present has existence. Tomorrow never comes. It is non-existent. It is death.

This would I teach: that money can be exchanged for nothing essential and of true value—for one cannot buy what is the property of the universe. Your mother, the earth, is no prostitute. You cannot buy of her.

Many a man, tangled in the snares of wealth, has thought to buy things—but found nothing for sale!

Wealth will buy a cloak to cover the back, yes—but what will cover the heart? And often, this is the uglier, and the colder.

Wealth will fill the belly—but the heart stays empty. And here are the greater hunger-pains. For the wealthiest are often the loneliest.

Know that a friend that is bought is not worth the price —regardless of the price. There can be no bargains here. Respect alone can gain a friend. But few indeed are the wealthy who can gain respect.

And the truth, for which you pretend to bargain so freely—is it the truth? No, it is flattery, else you would not buy!

O you worshipers of Mammon! How I pity you, and the ones whom you have deluded with your hypocrisy and false promises!

Sad indeed are the convictions of him who must lie unto others in order to convince himself.

Slaves! That is your proper name—for you see only the utilitarian and money-making aspect of your work, whatever you may do!

And let it be known that the most abject of all slaves are those who have sold themselves!

But in the Garden of the Heart, there are no slaves, because there is no work. Each plays at what he does, for each is free. He lives in the present, nor hoards for a nonexistent future. And living so, he finds that life is an art, a dance, and a laugh on the summer winds!

Man is not basically a competitive animal. His survival, as a race, has always depended more upon cooperation, one with another, than upon competition. No other animals compete with each other to the point of destroying their basic values in life.

Lo! In this temple there are many men. But the wealthy are few in number. Yet, all grovel for money!

Most of the worshipers of Mammon are in poverty. Their religion has set false values. And let this be known —that the greatest poverty on earth is in the temple of Mammon!

A poverty of the purse can be endured, and a man is often the stronger for it. But a poverty of the heart—truly, this is the lot of the most wretched!

Yes, you want your gold in the hand, rather than the heart—and for this reason are your hearts empty.

That evil taste within your mouths—it comes of licking pennies!

You who desire so much—it is your desires themselves which you love, and not the things or the money that buys them. That is why fulfillment so often brings disillusion and discontent.

Do not ask, "How can I be happy when I need this, or that, and something else?" Poverty is a creation of wealth, and the poor do not recognize themselves as such until envy creeps into their eyes.

He who has not seen a thing cannot covet it. Thus, poverty is recognized only in relation to wealth.

And if you cannot enjoy the little you have, for what it is, and for what you are, what makes you think you could be happy with still more?

He who collects now, recollects later—and perhaps the belch will be worse than the bite.

A warlike tribe are you Mammonites! For the wild-eyed political reformer may plan the mass-murder of war, and the professional butcher may perform it—but the loot belongs to the Mammonite, and for this reason he is always ready and willing to finance a war.

Where you refuse your smallest coin for better living conditions for your fellow man, you gladly gamble all your wealth that he may die more efficiently.

And why do you so willingly pay for war? It is because the loot is great—it being so easy to strip the dead!

Were the profit removed, there would be no war—for the wealthy would not finance it, and neither would they enslave a lesser people!

It is truly pitiful that men, the highest form of matter, should kill each other in wars over tracts of land—dirt, the lowest form of matter.

O you pitiful ones! Throw down your hideous idol! Return unto the Garden of the Heart!

The day has finally come when life is no longer a struggle of man against nature—but rather, a struggle of man against the malice of man!

In the Garden of the Heart, there is no struggle—for here are all things to be found, and nothing to be bought.

Golden is every sunset in the Garden of the Heart, but the gold is free; there is emerald underfoot, and opal overhead. What man among you has such jewels?

Much can be done, even in this lateness of the day. We can destroy the weeds. We can untie Virtue from the altar of Mammon, and send in search of Love.

Let us bow our heads and place flowers on the grave of Honor—still may there come another such as he. And his sister, Hope, still weeping there—let us raise her to her feet.

Thus, having made an end of speaking, I cast my eyes about the temple. And lo! The running to and fro had ceased. I heard a great murmuring arise from the throng before Mammon, and it spread beyond the hall of mighty pillars.

And a great stone was lifted from my heart. "Surely," I said to myself, "they will leave off this idolatry, having heard the truth!"

And many were the eyes fixed upon me where I stood, awaiting an answer. But lo! I felt the steps of one behind me. Then did I turn—only to behold the aged woman who had once spoken of love. And thus she spoke again, as in a whisper:

"Once I knew Love, and for this reason I befriend you, O wise one. Flee for your life—run, while there is yet time! For today, they prepare another sacrifice—it is to be Wisdom!"

Whereupon, I gave her my blessing, and with bowed head, turned to go. And as I left, I heard another voice, which said: "No—let him go. It is not he. For this one is mad—quite mad!"

10

Last Song of Solomon

The fame of Solomon spread throughout the world—verily, even as far as Sheba, the vast palm-laden shores below the great sands.

Thus was it said—that Solomon, King of the North, possessed a seal giving him power over all the forces of nature.[116] He could cause fountains of molten metal to gush forth, and he could command the winds to carry him whithersoever he might wish to go.

Therefore, he knew many things unseen, for he spoke with the birds, and he spoke with the beasts, and all these heard and obeyed.

Now Sheba[117] was ruled over by a woman who was both beautiful and wise. And when she heard these tales told of Solomon, she assembled her ministers and ordered them to gather together a caravan for Judah.[118] For she was eager to make herself known of him, that he might instruct her in the powers whereby he controlled nature.

A daughter of ancient Ur,[119] wise in the ways of the spheres, she spent three nights in the star-towers of Sheba, then departed northwards toward Judah.

And the caravan with which she went contained five hundred talents of spices, a camel laden with precious stones, ivory and ebony from Ophir, and a hundred and twenty talents of gold.[120], [121] For all this she had gathered as gift for the king of Israel.

But Solomon knew of her coming by a bird of the sky,[122]

and he drove his chariot forth by the eastern gate to meet her.

He was clad in white and Tyrian purple, arrayed in splendour, and the sun glinted on the gold dust powdered in his hair.[123]

Thus went Solomon, two schoeni south of Zion, to the garden and the palace that were Etham.[124] And upon arriving there, he tethered his horses to await her coming.

It was the new moon of Ziv,[125] the beginning of the dry season, and the morning sun spread its blood over the three terraced pools. The wild tulip was in bloom, and the fragrance of the scarlet flower filled the air. Solomon saw these things, and his heart was made glad.

And so it came to pass that Sheba, coming out of Hebron[126] on her way to Zion, was greeted at the garden of Etham.

Her glory was that of the dawn, and Solomon stood before her, silent with wonder. Golden ear-drops hung with Egypt's emeralds, golden chains upon her ankles, and her tunic—inlaid with many colored threads—revealed the queen's body colored as the freshly carved ivory, and lovely to behold.

Now King Solomon had ever sought to gather unto himself all that was beautiful, and his eyes were fixed with the radiance of Sheba. Therefore, he commanded that all preparations be made in her honor.

So lime-fires were lighted whereon were thrown frankincense and fragrant woods, and torches were made in like manner and set about the rooms. The music of the halil and timbrel guided the feet of dancing girls, and fingers swept the ten-stringed nebels[127] till their tinkling blended with the laughter of the fountains.

And a couch was prepared for Sheba of the skin of the

deer, and the skin of the leopard, and the skin of the badger, and over all was a covering of finest tahash[128] skins.

And servants were sent to the vaulted caverns beneath the eastern end of the lowermost pool to fetch aged wines, dates, figs, wild honey, and the choicest of meats. And King Solomon laid himself down to a feast with Sheba.

That day, from sunrise unto sunrise, they remained at Etham—and on the following day departed thence unto Zion to witness the wonders of Solomon.[129]

And she beheld the House of Solomon, which was thirteen years in building, and it was covered with cedar above and upon the beams that lay on five-and-forty pillars, fifteen in a row; and the steps whereto were guarded with twelve lions cut from stone, and the throne wherein was of ivory covered with gold.[130]

For Solomon had a love for things that are strange. His house was paved with glass over a large pool, so that, when Sheba sought to enter, she thought it a lake of water, and she bared her legs.[131] Then, knowing her mistake, she marveled at the ingenuity of Solomon.

All these works did Sheba see, and more, for the greatness of the king surpassed even the rumors thereof. But her thoughts dwelt on other things, and she was not satisfied. Thus, she enquired of those matters unseen, longing to know the wisdom of Solomon.

And so Sheba spoke to Solomon in this wise: "Mighty are your deeds, O Israel, the fruits of which my eyes have seen. Wondrous are they to behold. But all is of the day, and a working of hands, and a building of buildings. Surely, there are matters above these—and thereamong do I reckon wisdom."

And the heart of Solomon grew heavy, and he answered her, saying: "Many are the wise who would have been ignorant had they listened to their teachers. Do you, then, want my opinions—though they are tattered by the years? Behold my works! They are more extensive!

"Opinions must be earned, else they cannot be upheld. They are uncreative, and the husk of another's thinking. Can one be pregnant with the child of another?

"Better a fool, your own fool, than the wise property of a stranger."

And Sheba was angered by such harsh words, and she took issue with him, replying:

Normally, he who apologizes for his opinions before stating them, can have no opinions worthy of the stating.

But you are bitter, and you are cynical—O my king—and there is no better proof of a depth of heart than cynicism.

Clean of heart is the cynic—for one cannot smell the filth of another unless he is clean himself.

I would say that every cynic dreams of greater things, else why should he be cynical of the things that are?

Only he who can picture a palace will hate the hovel in which he lives, and he alone will build a finer house.

And I would say the same about the skeptic—for he is a cynic in search. And if you are cynical, above all things, be also skeptical. Ask for proof, even of me.

And why should anyone dislike the person who asks for proof? If you are honest and have reasons for your belief, it gives you a chance to establish yourself. But for the foolish and dishonest, it digs a hole.

Be not so given to self-reproach, O Israel. It is a shaming of pride and a praising of vanity. For this is the pride of self-reproach—that when one blames himself, he feels above the blame of others.

Often have I seen pride hanged on the gallows, that vanity might be entertained.

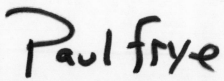

Humanity is a collection of individual selves. If everyone were self-sacrificing, all would be lost.

And Solomon was taken aback by these words from a woman. And he pondered over the wisdom which must prevail in the southlands—out of whose sands came Sheba. But he was bitter with the drouth of years, and he replied:

Let us not speak of humanity, even the few that may be self-sacrificing—for they are a soreness of heart and a dryness to my taste. Man is so ashamed of his own birth that his gods are begotten of virgins!

Man's inhumanity to man is seen primarily in his constant inhumanity to himself.

Pity the creature that is man. His mother fears his birth, and he fears his death. Beginning and ending in fear—yet his only pleasure is in escape from what he calls the 'humdrum of existence!'

Pity the creature that is man—for he is ashamed of himself. Does he not wear clothes?—clothes of the body, but mostly clothes of the mind. Only the blind hang a patch over the eye.

Man is the only animal among whose people the hatred of a brother has always been greater than the hatred of an enemy.

Pity the creature that is man. He enslaves the horse, but also enslaves himself. He despises the dog—yes, and his own brother. He is a parasite unto the cow, and how often a parasite unto his own kind! And in the end, the child of the plant he devours sends its roots into him!

Man is the only animal that is its own parasite. He defiles his body with that which is unclean and not good. He preys upon himself, and revels in his own downfall.

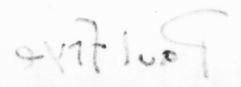

Pity the creature that is man—the only creature which deceives itself. He gives the blind a coin he has stolen from another, and then whispers in his own ear: 'I am kind.'

Man judges all things by himself. When he beholds that which is before him, he stares into a mirror casting back his own image. Too often he cries: 'Take it away! Take it away! It is ugly!'—Yet, he values himself above the image.

O Mother Earth! How your children have denied you! The sun is good, and they live in a cave and wear clothes. The air is good, and they build a door to their cave. Water is good, and the things of the soil are good—but the food and drink they often give their bodies, are shunned by the dogs they despise!

This creature called man—look upon him—how can it be hoped that he will learn to live!

And Sheba answered, saying: Man does not need to learn to live, for he is already living—but many need to recognize that they are alive.

Many are the walking dead who tread the earth in search of life—and unable to find it because they carry it with them, behind their backs.

When a man searches for his sword, and all the while it is strapped upon him, we say that he is absent-minded. But when one searches for a reason for living—even as yourself, O my king—and all the while he is alive, we do not call him absent-minded. We say that he is bitter, and cynical, and that he has forgotten how to laugh. And when he does laugh, it, too, is behind his back.

Our lives are temples wherein burn the fires of hopes, desires, dreams, ideals, and love—or whatever other names they may be called. When the fires are quenched, or are allowed to flicker out, the temple becomes a place of darkness and cold, forbidding, haunted—and soon beaten down by the elements.

Truly, there is selfishness in the human. But all things are selfish—because, in all things, the individual self is involved. Even to be known, things must be perceived through the human senses, and interpreted by the human self.

But merely because all things are interpreted through the individual self, does not mean that all things need be interpreted with selfishness alone—for in the human self, there is also love. And this it is which you have forgotten, O Israel!

In truth, one has ceased to love himself fully when he has ceased to extend himself in love toward others.

In the house of being, there are many windows, set at many angles. But only one looks out on the sunlight of the world beyond—and this is the window of love.

He who looks through other windows finds the outer world distorted and unreal, and he soon closes the casement out of fear, and dwells wholly within himself.

Each bears within himself a universe. But there is also a universe outside himself. When these two become different with the distortion of the inner world, a man falls out of harmony with the universe, and life becomes a twisting and a trouble.

And why is love the only window looking out on the sunlight of beyond? It is because love is a longingness, and an attraction, and a desire. To man himself it gives creativity, the well-spring of all things. It holds the inner world together with desire, and the outer with fulfillment.

* * * * * *

And upon hearing these words, Solomon the wise, the King of Israel, arose from the couch whereon he lay, and wonderment was written on his face—wonderment, and a shadow of doubt.

For how could it be that the universe, which contained all of the good, and all of the bad, and which dealt alike with both—how could it be orderly, and in harmony, and welded together with love? Could the night be possessed of the day, or the day of the night? For, in the darkness of his own mind, he saw not that day and night are but a naming of names—even as are good and bad.[132]

And the queen saw the bitterness that was in the heart of Solomon, and the cause thereof, and she spoke, saying:

"O Israel! Your thoughts are as wormwood to the taste. Even in Sheba it is known that an act is only an act, and it is further known that good and evil are but names having no part in the act.

"And this do I declare to you: that the one great characteristic of the universe is love, a holding together, an urge to create—and that you do not enquire wisely concerning this."

So it was that, during the night, Solomon found little sleep—for he meditated upon these things. And lo! A great heaviness lifted itself from his heart. For the first time, he beheld the universe as it is, and he became happy with this newly discovered truth.

And when the Queen of Sheba, who was known as Makeda, had departed again for those vast palm-laden shores below the great sands, Solomon sat in thought.

And the thoughts of Solomon were of the past—for he had been a bloody man, born of a bloody father, and he had been sickened by many wives. For Solomon had not known of love.

Verily, he had slain his own brother.[133] His kingdom was a pawn, his temple a kennel with slain men at the altar, the seat of his love a charnel house, and his Song the bubbling of flesh-pots!

Many strange women had he taken unto himself, for he had trafficked in flesh—seven hundred wives, princesses, and three hundred concubines.[134]

What knew Solomon of love? Though it is native to the flesh, it needs to be carefully tended. A great crime is dissipation, and the victim thereof is love.

All these things did Solomon consider, for this is a sequel to Solomon, to the thoughts of Solomon, and the Song of Solomon. It is an echo from the deep well of centuries—a returning of words upward out of the blackness.

For Solomon mused all alone, one dusk, under the fronds of a palm which grew in the Garden of Etham. And this was his song, his last song—the thousand-and-fifth:

Weary am I of the daughter of Egypt. Though comely, she is not of my love. Weary am I of the women of Acco, and the dancers—yea, even the palace carvings of women. For these are not of my love.

For my beloved is a dream and a vision of youth. Her eyes are as deep and as dark as the three terraced pools of my garden.

Like the dark-spotted tails of the peacocks of Ophir, are her eyes. Yea, like unto a white peacock is she. Beautiful is my beloved.

In that hour between sunset and star-rise, she bringeth herself unto me. On the softest and stillest of feet doth she enter my garden—and she trembleth and is afraid.

O come, my beloved! Be not afraid, for the night is a
child, and the water of night still wetteth the grasses, and
the lamps of the night are unlit.

A thousand and five are my songs for thee, but the harp-
strings of my heart still quiver in thy love.

For thou art a skin of wine to my senses. Thy kisses are
wild honey to my mouth, and thy body is as smooth and as
white as the tusks of the beasts from Ophir.

Lo! In the depths of the moonless night, my beloved
bringeth herself unto me—unto my couch doth she come,
and I am happy for her coming.

She weareth a veil of white engirdled with fine jewels.
White as the unleavened bread is her skin, and the sunlets
that rise on her breast are of gold. Altogether beautiful is
my beloved—yea, a nether-stone in the mill of my desire.

Beautiful is my beloved, for she is a dream and a vision
of youth. She is purer than the waters of Siloam,[135] than
the Fountain of the Virgin, which is in the Eastern Valley.

In her name, at En-gedi,[136] I built me a garden, and this
one at Etham—two schoeni south of Zion; sealed its fountains, slew the wild unicorn, and felled the olive and the
lote tree.

And so, I have raised her a palace—a palace of marble
from quarries that lay by the gate to Damascus.

And when the rains are all gone, and the Moon of
Adar[137] has come, vines trail from the flat roof of the palace
through the open lattice of my window.

For my soul looketh out like a window on a garden of
pleasures, and my love is a vine, heavy with fruit, stealing
into my chamber. She is decked with flowers and en-
twineth my heart with tendrils.

Yea, when the second watch is beaten on the great

bronze gong in the vault beneath the palace garden, my beloved cometh unto me, and the tinkling of her ankle ornaments marks her coming.

Dark are her eyes—as a javelin in my heart, for she is a dream and a vision of youth. A talent is she in heaviness, a cubit of waist, and more lovely than the jewels of Tarshish[138] or the fountains of En-gedi, and she is mine.

She weareth a veil of white, and a mantle of blue dyed with the blood of the shellfish, and these are cast aside.

A tunic of fine linen doth she wear, embroidered with figures of Tyre, engirdled with a golden image of the burning serpent, Nahash[139], [140]—and these are cast aside.

At the door of my chamber doth she unloose the jeweled latchet of her sandals of badger skin, and she approacheth my couch cloaked only in her flowing locks—for she is mine.

I am Solomon, King of all Israel, from Tipsah unto Gaza,[141] but none have I seen like unto her!

Beautiful art thou, O my beloved! More beautiful than the moonlight over Carmel.[142]

Much flesh have I known, but never such as thine. Many images have I raised in the valley about Moriah,[143] but never one of thy loveliness.

Thy features, O thou whom my soul owneth, are the blossoms out of Sharon,[144] and the birds about the rivers. How glad is my heart at our coming together!

Thy thighs, O my desired one, are as of marble never touched by hammer, the whiteness whereof is of milk.

How graceful art thou—a reed upon the Kidron,[145] a breeze among the rushes, a waving of summer grasses where no foot hath trodden.

Thy breath is the breath of the dawn. Soft and firm are thy breasts as lily buds of the same stalk, and the movements of thy body are the music of the timbrel and the kinnor to my senses.

Beautiful art thou, O my beloved! Thy belly is a lotos from the pools of Asher,[146] thine eyes are Egypt's emeralds, and thy voice is that of bulbul[147] in the thickets of the Jordan.

Thou stirrest my blood, O thou whom my soul owneth— thou stirrest my blood till my desire burneth like the lime- fires that burn in the belly of Molech.[148]

Yea, as a fire throughout the cedars, dost thou sweep into my heart, and the world is made light by thee, and the altars of my love are lighted in thy flame.

Wheresoever thou goest, there shall I go after thee. Wheresoever thou seekest to hide, Song of my Heart, there shall I seek thee out—for thou art mine.

A flower art thou, O my sweet one, a flower with the petals still unopened, a fruit the skin whereof is whole, a tree whence no leaf hath fallen.

Thou goest down into the garden, and the grasses bow to thee, and the winds have sung to thee, and brought thee odors of musk and spices.

Mournful is the call of the doves that nest in the lattice, when thou art gone, and the darkness of the night is that of death, and of many waters all is weeping.

Long hours through the night hath my bed-candle wept its tears of wax that thou hast not blessed its light.

Return! O come back, my beloved! Let my heart feast upon thee. For thou art a wind through the palms, a palace in the sands, and rare fruits to the mouth that hath long hungered.

Sacred art thou to my soul—for did I not find thee on the seventh day of the seventh moon, which is Ethanim, in the weeks of years?

Sacred art thou to me. Thy fruits are my fruits, and thy body my body—for thou art a dream and a vision whence none could wish to waken.

Behold! Late rains from the moon of Adar drip from the vines on the palace roof, tinkling as a thousand harp-strings, and add their weight to the three terraced pools of my garden.

So art thou to me, my beloved. Thou drivest the hot south wind from my heart. Thou refreshest the grasses of my youth, and addest thy beauty to the depths of my being.

Yea, when thou dancest before me, I am afire for thee. I have learned thy footsteps in the garden, and watched the moonrise for thy coming.

For I am a vineyard heavy with honey of grapes, and I wait for the tread of thy feet.

Have I not built for thee a garden that I might lie among the flowers with thee, that we might together pluck the lotos from the pools?

O my beloved! Thou art fertile as the fig that is ripe throughout the year, as the land of Sharon that needeth not the water.

Thy arms are about me, thy breasts against me, and thy mouth upturned as the blossom of the hyssop that asketh for the plucking.

Thou takest my breath and lightest a fire in me—as the fire that burneth in the belly of Molech, that standeth on the high place which is Tophet, in the valley that is Hinnom.

Thou lightest a fire in me, and thy breath is the incense before Baal and Asherah!

O my beloved, be not afraid—for the night is a child, and the water of night still wetteth the grasses, and the lamps of the night are unlit. It neareth the hour of the first watch.

All night have I lain with thee, my beloved. The stringed music of dripping water, from the palace vines, hath stopped. The sound of the last watch, beaten on the bronze gong in the vaults beneath the palace garden, echoeth through the moonlight, and dieth out.

Thou art gone! Thou art vanished from my chamber! Whither art thou fled, O my beloved? I have shouted from my chariot throughout Zion, I have ridden over Carmel, and swept the cane-brake from the Kidron. But thou art nowhere to be found!

Pure is my desired one, as the Fountain of the Virgin, which is in the Eastern Valley. Her body is my body, her fruit my fruit, for she is *of* me—a dream and a vision of youth.

A dream is she, and a vision of youth. But never shall I find her. Of a thousand women, she is numbered not among them.

A dream is she, and a vision of youth. But I shall find her not—for I am unfit to be taken unto her!

I am Solomon, king of all Israel from Tipsah unto Gaza. My mother's children made me keeper of the vineyards, but mine own vineyards have I not kept—for I have battened on flesh—and my heart is only a bag of blood!

Thus sang Solomon, one moonless night, under the fronds of a palm that grew in the garden of Etham, south of the city of David, which is Zion.

And of further words, little is known. But it has been related that, when the death of Solomon had been decreed, nothing revealed his death but a worm of the earth—

Shameer—which gnawed down the staff that supported his corpse. And when it fell, the Djinn stood silent in their wonder, feeling strange that they were freed from their slavery unto him![149]

Did Solomon say that all is vanity and a striving after winds? Then I say unto Solomon that the rose is beautiful, but he who blinds himself speaks only of thorns!

Notes and References

City of the Horizon

1. The god, *Aton* was probably of Syrian origin, though there is an older Egyptian form, *Atum*. Akhnaton had Syrian blood in him through his mother, Tiy, and the name of the Syrian god was *Adon*, known in the Greek form as *Adonis*.

2. The line here quoted is the final sentence in a small prayer found engraved on the gold foil beneath the feet of the coffin containing the mummy of Akhnaton; trans. from the hieroglyphic Egyptian by Gardiner.

3. *Akhnaton*, Amenhotep IV, Amenophis IV, reigned in Egypt from 1375 B.C. to 1358 B.C., in which year he died of dysostosis. He founded a new religion, Atonism, the symbol for which was the sun. It was the world's first monotheism.

4. In order to get away from the Theban priesthood of Amenism, Pharaoh Akhnaton moved the capital of Egypt from Thebes downstream to the present site of the village of Tell el-Amarna, about 190 miles from Cairo. He built a city there and named it *Akhetaton*, "the City of the Horizon." It was set on a small plateau where the eastern hills receded some three miles from the Nile, and was extremely beautiful.

5. *Maru-Aton* was a "paradise" or pleasure ground built south of the city of Akhetaton near the modern village of Hawata. It consisted of artificial lakes, temples, etc.

6. *Nefertiti*, "The Beautiful One Comes," was the wife of Akhnaton, and one of the world's loveliest women. She probably helped with the sunset rites of Aton, for she is mentioned in the hieroglyphs in the tomb of Ay, her father, as: "She who sends the Aton to rest with a sweet voice, and her two beautiful hands bearing two systrums."

7. *Hatshepsut*, wife of Thutmose III (great grandfather of Akhnaton) took a long voyage to the land of Punt—from which she brought back many strange treasures wherefrom she built her famous

133

terraced myrrh-gardens.

8. The *Ankh*, or "crux ansata," was a small cross, and was a symbol of life. It is a quite frequent figure found in the Akhnaton period.

9. Tutankhamen, originally named Tutankhaton, and the son-in-law of Akhnaton, later moved the capital back to Thebes, leaving the City of the Horizon deserted. Following the death of Akhnaton, the Theban priesthood of Amenism destroyed or removed everything of value.

10. Contrary to popular belief, the Egyptians were a very happy people. As an old Egyptian banquet song, from the hieroglyphic, has it: "Increase yet more the desires that thou hast, and let not thine heart grow faint. Follow thy desires, and do good to thyself. Do whatever thou requirest upon the earth—but vex not thine heart." Also: "Follow thine heart so long as thou livest, and do not more than is said. Diminish not the time wherein thou followest the heart, for this is abhorrent unto it." Hieroglyphics of *The Proverbs of Ptah-hotep*, No. IX. Ptah-hotep was vizier to the Pharaoh Esesi, 27th Century, B.C.

Land of the Seven Terraces

11. *Svetaketu* is a figure taken from the *Khandogya Upanishad*, trans. from the Sanskrit by Max Mueller, *Sacred Books of the East*. However, the story given here is highly embellished, being somewhat parallel to the story of Siddhartha Gautama, lord Buddha. Some of the figures of speech are drawn from the *Buddha-Karita* of Asvaghosha. The philosophy itself is from many ancient Indian sources, including virtually all the Vedanta.

12. *Kshatriyas*. The ruling caste of India, concerned with control of worldly affairs, and second only to the Brahmin caste, which controlled spiritual affairs.

13. Originally, the people of India were quite blonde—being of the same stock as the ancient Greeks. However, after migrating through the Khaibar and Bolan passes of the Himalayas, they found a black-skinned aboriginal tribe, the Dravidians, living to the south. As the centuries passed, they finally intermixed with these. Thus, the caste system was born. An individual's caste indicated roughly the degree of white versus black strains in his heritage. The Sanskrit word for caste is "Varna." It means, translated, nothing more than "color." The English word "varnish" is a derivative of the basic root of this Sanskrit term. The skin of the lord Buddha (Siddhartha Gautama), who was born of the Kshatriya caste in 568 B.C., was described by his chief disciple, Ananda, as being the color of freshly carved ivory.

14. *Himavat* was a rich and highly forested area in the Punjab of northern India. It is possibly identical with the small principality from which Gautama came.

15. *The Land of Seven Terraces* is probably a mythical kingdom in northern India. But, inasmuch as it figures often in the more ancient Indian literature, it may have had some reference to an actual place at one time.

16. *Mount Kailasa* is one of the larger peaks of the Himalayas. It is fabled for its beauty, and also has considerable religious significance.

17. *The Temple of the Tortoise* was a beautiful structure in the area of Kalinga, India.

18. The *yogana* is an Indian measure of distance quite similar to the English mile.

19. The *Brikshu* is a religious beggar, dressed in red, and required to obtain all his food by begging.

20. *Shiva*, a figure often referred to in this volume. Shiva is one of the great Hindu trinity. In the Vedas, the word Shiva is an epithet for Rudra, a personification of the storms and wilder forces of nature. In the Puranic period, Shiva became identical with the Supreme Being. Later, Shiva became a symbol for love, and as Nataraja, symbolized the rhythm and orderliness of all things. Thus, Shiva Nataraja is pictured as a dancing god—symbolizing the rhythm of the universe and all that it contains. Tayumanavar says: "Oh thou that dancest the dance of bliss in the Hall of Consciousness!" Ultimately, this dance—the best known form of Shiva —was probably derived from the Aryan Rudra, and in almost all Shiva temples there is a special dancing hall, or *Natana-sabha*, dedicated to Nataraja. The most ancient or sacred of these is at Tillai. The vast significance of the dance of Shiva runs throughout all the ancient literature. Thus, in the *Tiruvatavurar Purana*, Shiva is described: "Our Lord is the Dancer who, like the heat latent in firewood, diffuses his power in mind and matter, and makes them dance in their turn." And again, in the *Cidambara Mummani Kovai*: "Oh, my Lord, thy hand which holds the sacred drum has ordered and made rhythmic the heavens and earth and other worlds. Thy lifted hand protects both the animate and inanimate extended universe." But the dance of Shiva does not symbolize only the universe, but all the living things as well—including the human, and even his thoughts. In the *Tiru-Arul-Payan*, we read: "The dance of nature proceeds on one side, the dance of wisdom on the other." As a matter of fact, the third eye on Shiva icons is the eye of wisdom.

21. The *Rita* is the "Law" of which Varuna is the keeper, the immuta-

ble ordinances that he established and maintains. They represent the order and rhythm of the cosmos, regulating "the motions of the sun and the moon and the stars, the alternations of day and night, of the seasons, the gathering of the waters in clouds and their downpour in rain; in short, the order that evolves harmony out of Chaos, and the visible scene of whose working is the sky. . . . There is a moral *Rita*, as there is a material one, or rather, the same Rita rules both worlds. What Law is in the physical, that Truth, Right, is in the spiritual order, and both are Rita." Zenaide A. Ragozin, *The Story of Vedic India*, V, 12. G. P. Putnam's Sons' ed., 1895, p. 146.

That *Rita* means cosmic order is portrayed in the word itself, which means "keep the world going." The Sanskrit root, Ri, means "to flow" and we find it in the Greek, Rheo, and in the English words: *river. rite, ri*tual. In the *Rig-Veda*, X, 85, we read: "Through the law (Rita) the earth stands firm, the Heavens and the Sun, through the law the Adityas stand, and Soma stands in the sky."

22. *Love* (Kama) is fundamental to the philosophy of the Vedanta. It is the basis of the Rita, and its essential rhythmic nature is symbolized by Shiva Nataraja. In fact, it is looked upon as the superstructure of the universe and all that it contains, both animate and inanimate. In the justly famous Cosmogonic Hymn (X, 129 of the *Rig-Veda*) we read of the early Indian concept of the creation of all things, and verses three and four state: "In the beginning, there was darkness in darkness enfolded. And all was undistinguishable abyss. That One (Sat, Ekham) which lay in empty space, wrapped in nothingness, was developed by the power of heat. Then desire arose in It (love, Kama)—that was the primal germ of mind, which poets, searching with their intellects, discovered to be the bond between being and non-being." Cf. also *Rig-Veda*, X. 121. The best translation of *Rig* hymn X, 129, from which the above is quoted, is to be found in the German of Adolph Kaegi, *Rig Veda*, published in two parts: *Wissenschaftliche Beilage zum Programm der Kantonschule in Zürich*, 1878–1879.

Millenniums of the Lordly Stars

23. *Alborz*, or Elburz, is called "Hara-Berezaita" in the *Zend-Avesta* of ancient Persia, and is said to be the center of the world, and the mother of mountains. Cf. *Vendidad*, Fargard XXI, 5, in Darmesteter's trans. of the *Zend-Avesta*, *Sacred Books of the East*. Cf. also *Bundahish*, XX, 4.

24. The city referred to is Shiz, Chiz, Gaznah, Gazn, Gandzag, and is thought by Jackson to be the present ruins of Takht-i-Suleiman.

25. There is good reason to associate Afrasyab with this city and region. In a Pahlavi work of the ninth century A.D., we find: "Frasiak of Tur (Afrasyab) founded the town of Ganjak (Shiz)." *Shatroiha-i-Airan*, trans. by Modi, p. 117. Firdausi, in his *Shahnamah*, IV, 196, speaks of a cave on a mountain, near Barda, where Afrasyab hid. But in the older legend (*Bundahish*, XII, 20) it was a palace of a hundred columns—its height a thousand times that of a man. Cf. also *Aogemaide Nask*, 61–64, of Darmesteter's trans. of the *Zend-Avesta*.

26. In Persian, *mahin cherkh*, "the great cycle," in Arabic, *dawrah-i kabra*. It supposedly symbolizes the cyclic nature of all things, and therefore their immortality. *Avissenna*, or *Avicenna*, whose full name was *Abu Ali Hussain Ben Abdallah, ben Sina, al Shaikh al ra'is*, known to the Arabs as *Ibn Sina*, and to the jews as *Arabisans Aben Sina*, says: "Every form and image, which seems gone at present, is safely stored in the treasury of time. When the same positions of the heavens occur once more, each shall be brought out from behind the mysterious veil." The *Hakim Umr Khakani* says: "Those who adorn the heavens, which are a particle of time, come and depart again, reappear on the same stage. For in the skirts of heaven, and the robes of earth, there is a creation which is successively born as long as Ormuzd (the universe) lives." And the *Mulla Suffi of Ispahan* says: "This revolution of time is like unto a painted lantern which, notwithstanding its motion, remains in the same position." Mohsan Fani, *The Dabistan*, trans. by Shea & Troyer, p. 189. Cf. also *Rig-Veda*, X, 14, 1–2; Pliny, *Natural History*, II, 1; *Mahabharata, Bhagavad Gita*, Chap. VIII; and *Also Sprach Zarathustra*, Neitzsche, III, 46, 2.

27. Nizami, the Persian poet, wrote of the love of Khosru Parviz for a beautiful Armenian princess, *Shirin*, also loved by Farhad, a sculptor. Khosru was, as a ruler, noted for his luxurious habits and his defiance of Allah.

28. "*Laili*, in beauty, softness, grace, surpassed the loveliest of her race." Nizami, *Romance of Laili and Majnun*, trans. by Atkinson.

29. The *Amoo* was a river of ancient Persia.

30. *Zal* was a hero of Persian legend, and celebrated by many Persian authors for his great feats of bravery. He was set apart from the rest of mankind by reason of his great abundance of long snow-white hair.

31. *Khizer* was the legendary Persian prophet who discovered and drank from the Fountain of Life. It was he who offered the cup of immortality to Hafiz al Shirazi, one of the greatest lyric poets of Persia.

The Peach-blossom Fountain

32. *Tao Chien* (Tao Yuan-ming) was one of the many versatile writers of ancient China. He was born in 365 A.D. and died in 427 A.D. He was a minor government official, and rather than work for cheap wages, he went into seclusion and lived the life of a scholar. His chief pastime was raising wild chrysanthemums. His *Peach-blossom Fountain* is a well known allegory, and is adapted for the basis of this story.

33. *Cheng*—a musical instrument of ancient China, having twelve metal strings; it is somewhat similar to a lute in construction.

34. *Mao Yen Shou*—a painter, chiefly of porcelain, the delicacy of whose work has become legendary.

35. *Lady Li*—a legendary figure often found in Chinese literature. She was noted for her many graces and her beauty.

36. *Spirit-screen*—Evil spirits can travel only in straight lines. Thus, a screen is placed before the door for protection, since they would then be unable to enter in a straight-line path. Compare this device with the imperfect pentagram that allowed Mephistopheles into Faust's study, but would not let him out again. (Goethe's *Faust*, Act I, Scene III.)

37. The Master, *Kung*, is Chinese idiom for Confucius.

38. "All that we are is a result of what we have thought: it is founded upon our thoughts, it is made up of our thoughts." *The Dhammapada Sutra*, Chap. I, 1; trans. from the Pali by Max Mueller, *Sacred Books of The East.*

39. "Only the truly intelligent know the unity of all things. They therefore do not make distinctions, but follow the common and ordinary." *Chuang Tzu*, Chap. II, p. 52; trans. from the Chinese by Dr. Yu-Lan Fung, Shanghai, 1933. Also: "The common and the ordinary are the natural functions of all things, which express the common nature of the whole. Following the common nature of the whole, they are happy. Being happy, they are near perfection." *Ibid.* p. 52. In his *Philosophy of Human Nature,* Chu Hsi mentions a statement of Li Fang-Shu: "To be one with all things in the universe," he said, "is love." Chu Hsi, *The Philosophy of Human Nature,* trans. by J. P. Bruce, p. 321. Inasmuch as Taoism, according to Lao Tzu and his disciple Chuang Tzu, involves a monistic view of the universe, it is identified with the principles that make the universe orderly and rhythmic, and therefore can be identified with love. Thus, in Ssu-k'ung T'u, we find: "Behold the mighty axis of the earth, the moving pole of the skies! Let us observe their ways and become one with them—beyond the limits

of thought, circling forever an endless orbit of years throughout the stretching void! Yea, this is the key to Tao." Ssu-k'ung T'u, a Taoist poet, A.D. 834–908; trans. by H. Giles, in his *Chinese Literature*. In modern times Lin Yu Tang has said: "What we need above all is a theory of the rhythm of life, and of the unity and interrelatedness of all things. Without that faith, the doctrine of force cannot be destroyed." Lin Yu Tang, *Between Tears and Laughter*, John Day Co., 1943, p. 59. Cf. also Confucius, *Doctrine of the Mean*, XXX.

40. Meng Tzu, Disciple of Confucius, has said: "The great man is he who does not lose his child's heart." *Meng Tzu*, Bk. IV, XII, 1.

41. "Illusion is the most interesting thing in the world; without illusion, there would be no pleasure." And again: "The very thought that things are important, is itself an illusion." *Kurozumi-Kyo-Kyo-Sho*, Vol. 1, p. 47, poem 117; *Ibid.*, p. 50, poem 126. Trans. by C. W. Hepner, *The Kurozumi Sect of Shinto*, Tokyo, 1935.

Lesson of the Stone

42. *Accensus*—public servant who proclaims the time of day, or the hour of the watch at night.

43. *Galen* was a famous physician and pharmacist from Pergamum in Asia Minor. A.D. 130–200.

44. *Marcus Aurelius* and *Lucius Verus* were co-emperors of Rome at this time. Their reign, and particularly the year 166 A.D., was one of the greatest turning-points in the history of the world. In this year, the great plague began—the plague which most historians regard as the beginning of the end of Rome. (Cf., Reinhold Niebuhr *Lectures on the History of Rome*, Vol. III, p. 251.) In the reign of Aurelius, moreover, Christianity emerged from the cellars of Rome and became a topic of public and literary discussion. Prosperity also ended with his reign, and tyranny set in. Commodus set the example later followed. Philosophy underwent a similar change—for Aurelius marked the high-point of stoicism.

45. *Vologeses* was the Asiatic emperor conquered by Rome, and from battles with whom the army returned in 166 A.D.

46. The *Temple of Peace*, containing lecture halls and a library, was founded by Vespasian, and was a popular literary resort at the time.

47. *Cornelius Fronto* was the best known teacher of Marcus, during his youth. He was born at Cirta, in Numidia, during the reign of Domitian.

48. *Q. Junius Rusticus,* an austere stoic, who superseded Fronto as teacher of Marcus. He introduced Marcus to the *Discourses* of Epictetus.

49. Cf. *Meditations,* Marcus Aurelius, IX, 35, and IV, 23.

50. *Ibid.,* II, 9, and VIII, 14.

51. Marcus has said: "Nothing is evil which is according to nature." *Meditations,* VII, 3. This view is quite similar to that held by Seneca. Cf. his *Epistolae,* Ep. LXXVI, 15. Marcus Aurelius, however, seemed to feel that everything that was according to nature was thereby good. *Meditations,* IV, 10. This was also the opinion of several other stoics. On the other hand, Epictetus felt that evil itself was necessary for the harmony of the whole: ". . . abundance and scarcity, and virtue and vice, and all such opposites for the harmony of the whole." *Discourses,* Bk. I, Chap. XII. In *Gellius,* VI, 1, from Bk. IV of Chrysippus on Providence, we find: "Nothing is more foolish than the opinions of those who think that good could have existed without evil." But Simplicius argues, rightfully enough, in his commentary on the *Encheiridion* of Epictetus, that if there were a principle of evil in all things, then it would no longer be evil, but good. Cf. also *Boethius,* Chap. XI, 1, King Alfred's Anglo-Saxon Version.

52. Cf. Seneca, *Dialogues,* Bk. IV, Chap. IX, 1.

53. Thrasea has said: "He that hates vice hates mankind." Pliny, *Epistolae,* XXII, Bk. VIII, Sect. 3. Thrasea Paetus was a stoic philosopher who, in Nero's time, was ordered to put himself to death. (Tacitus, *Annals,* XVI, 21)

54. The days of the Antonines, of which Marcus was the last, were the happiest days of the Roman Empire. Gibbon says: "If a man were called to fix the period in the history of the world during which the condition of the human race was most prosperous and happy, he would, without hesitation, name that which elapsed from the death of Domitian to the accession of Commodus." Edward Gibbon, *The Decline and Fall of the Roman Empire,* Vol. I, Chap. III.

55. *Aesculapius* was the Roman god of medicine. (Greek: *Asclepius*)

Lament of Babylon

56. *Nabonidus* was the last king of Babylon. Babylon fell on Tammuz 16th, 539 B.C.

57. For the fertility of the plains of Shinar, upon which the city was built, cf. Herodotus, I, 178–180; Diodorus, II, 95–96; and Quintus Curtius, V, 1.

58. *Nisaba* was goddess of vegetation, and her breasts were the hills covered with vegetation. *Ki wood,* black—probably ebony.

59. This bridge was thirty feet wide, and three thousand and three hundred feet long, according to Diodorus. However, Strabo, XVI, 738, says that the Euphrates itself was only a furlong (approx. 660 feet) in breadth.

60. The *Tower of Babel* consisted of eight levels, one above the other, topped by the temple of Seven Spheres—probably a temple to Ishtar. Strabo compares it to a pyramid. However, it was higher than any pyramid. Cf. Herodotus, I, 181; Diodorus, II, 98. It is interesting to note that the Mayans, who also built terraced towers, declare in the Tzental legend of Votan, that this hero, enroute to Valum Chivim, passed by the ancient tower that had been built to climb the sky, and where God had given each tribe its language!

61. *Gubba* stones, precious stones, variety unknown.

62. *Indus*—a river of India. Babylon carried on commerce this far.

63. *Semiramus*—an earlier queen of Babylon. It was she who built the reservoir into which Ugbaru, commanding the legions of Cyrus of Persia, drew off the waters of the Euphrates in order to march up the river bed and take over Babylon. She was fond of raising doves.

64. *Sennacherib,* the Assyrian, pillaged Babylon in 689 B.C. As for the scorpion men, and the monster, Lakhamu, cf. *The Story of Creation,* Cuneiform Tablets, Tablet II, 25–30.

65. The belly of *Tiamat* (the world) was torn open at the birth of the earth. Cf. *The Story of Creation,* Cuneiform Tablets, Tablet IV, lines 95–105.

66. The famous *Hanging Gardens* of Babylon were built by Nebuchadnezzar for his wife, Amytis, a Median, who longed for the more luxurious vegetation of her home country. They stood in the "new" palace on the west side of the river, and were built in terraces, supported by arches, one above the other, being 400 feet on the side at the base. Cf. Diodorus, II, 98–99; Strabo, XVI, 738, and Quintus Curtius, V, 1.

67. *Ushu* and *ukarinu* woods were precious woods, possibly used for the making of incense, and often listed with the booty taken by the kings.

68. *Uknu* stones were precious stones whose nature is unknown. Yellow *sea-clay* was amber.

69. *Ishtar,* the goddess of love and fertility, entered hell each spring in search of her mate, Tammuz. In the process of entering, she was completely stripped. At the first gate, she relinquished her

crown, at the second, her earrings, and so on until she was naked after the seventh gate. It will be recalled that, in the Greek, Charon's passengers were always stripped. Cf. *Epic of Ishtar and Izdubar,* "Ishtar's Descent to Hades," trans. from the cuneiform by Jeremias.

Ishtar can be identified with Venus, and she was considered the daughter of Sin—the moon god of Ur. She is the Ashtart of the Phoenicians, the Astarte of the Greeks, and the Ashtoreth of the Canaanites. These latter, who hated Ishtar, suffixed "eth" to her name, from the word "bosheth," meaning shame.

70. The *asherim* were the cone-shaped phallic symbols of Ishtar. The temple incidents of enforced (though willing) prostitution of maidens prior to marriage—made notorious by Herodotus (I, 199) —are very likely exaggeration. Cf. Jastrow, *Religion in Babylonia and Assyria,* pp. 137–42. It is difficult to believe that a land that produced the laws of Hammurapi could undergo such a moral revolution. For example, this monarch decreed: "If the wife of a man be taken lying with another man, they shall bind them together, and throw them into the water to drown."—from the Cuneiform, *Laws of Hammurapi,* Law 129, Reverse of Col. V.

71. *Marduk* was the principle deity of Babylon. It was the priests of Marduk, assisted by the captive Jews, who betrayed Babylon. At a prearranged hour, during the feast in celebration of the return of Ishtar from Hell (Tammuz 16th), they opened the great gates leading to the quays on the Euphrates—the river that ran through the center of the city. Thus, Ugbaru, in command of the legions of Cyrus of Persia, drained the river off into the reservoir of Semiramus, marched up the river bed, was admitted to the city, and conquered it without so much as a single clash of arms.

72. *Sarbatu wood* was an odoriferous wood used for incense.

In The House of Aspasia

73. *Apollo* was the deity of youth and beauty, also of music, poetry, and the oracles. He sent and stopped the plagues, was god of healing, and the twin of Artemis. In later times he was identified with Helios, the sun God.

74. *Aspasia* was a famous courtesan of Athens, about whom there is a liberal account to be found in Plutarch's *Lives.* The courtesan of that time was not, in the strict sense, a prostitute. Rather, they were skilled in knowledge and the social graces, and were adept at entertainment—much in the fashion of the Geisha girls of Japan. Their houses were meeting places for the learned and literary people of the times. In the case of Aspasia, she was a favorite of

Pericles, who ruled Athens, as well as the famous Socrates, Alcibiades, Phidias, and many others.

75. The *Olympiad* was a period of five years between and including the feast year of Apollo. Greek chronology began with the year 776 B.C. The eighty-fourth Olympiad, in which this story is set, is a date taken from Plutarch, but would, by calculation, appear to be later than the dates normally given for the life of Pericles (495–429 B.C.)

76. *Panenus* was famous for his mosaics. He was a brother of the famous sculptor *Phidias*, and lived with him in Periclean Athens. *Callicrates* was a sculptor second in fame only to Phidias, and lived at the same time.

77. *Bacchus* was god of revelry and drink. He was often symbolized, fittingly enough, by snakes and grapes.

78. *Thargelia* was another courtesan also famed for her wisdom and beauty. Cf. Plutarch, *Life of Pericles*.

79. *Damon* was a musician of the period, *Sappho* was a lyric poetess from Lesbos, and *Sophocles* and *Euripides* were playwrights. *Alcibiades*, who also lived at this time, was a politician and general.

80. *The Cyprian* was the goddess, Diana, who frequently was depicted as a huntress, particularly after she was identified with Artemis and worshiped as a moon goddess.

81. *Hyperion* was a titan, father of the sun, and later identified with Apollo.

82. *Dionysus*—another name for Bacchus.

83. *Empedocles* was a philosopher who lived about 500–430 B.C. Though he was not a native of Athens, he could well have gone there on visits. Cf. John Burnet, *Early Greek Philosophy*, p. 203. *Zeno*, of Elea, another philosopher, lived about the same time (475 B.C.). For the best translations of these men, cf. Diels, *Die Fragmente der Vorsokratiker*, Vol. 1, p. 220 ff.

84. Athens actually was in religious turmoil at that time. People were losing faith in the old gods of the city, and many new ones were being imported from Asia Minor and Egypt. This religious disintegration was furthered by the natural skepticism that came with advancing knowledge. This situation, rather than any actual teachings, accounts for the indictment and execution of Socrates, who was said to be corrupting the youth of the city.

85. Little is known of the actual death of Empedocles. He is said to have cried out: "All hail! Oh friends! But unto you I walk as god immortal now, no more as man!"—and then leaped into the crater of Etna. This statement is translated by William Ellery Leonard.

Cf. his *The Fragments of Empedocles,* Fragment 112, p. 53. However, Empedocles may have meant something else, for we do not have the context of the statement. Burnet says: "We are told that Empedokles of Akragas leapt into the crater of Etna that he might be deemed a god. This appears to be a malicious version of a tale set on foot by his adherents that he had been snatched up to heaven in the night." John Burnet, *Early Greek Philosophy,* p. 202.

The Unwritten Sura of Mohammed

86. This incident is related in the *Hanifs,* the commentaries to the Koran, and probably actually occurred. Who knows what Mohammed so wanted to record in that strange half light of impending death? This refusal to allow him writing materials, made by his son-in-law, Omar, brought about a noisy quarrel, and Mohammed ordered the group from the room. Mohammed's request, as quoted here, was translated by Dermenghem.

87. *Omar* was the second Caliph. *Abu Bekr* was the first Caliph (following to power after the death of Mahomet.) His daughter, Aisha, was the Prophet's favorite wife.

88. *Azrael* was the angel of death.

89. *Khadija* was the first wife of Mohammed, and probably also his first convert. She played a very important role in his advancement in that she had the necessary wealth to promote his endeavors. She owned a large caravan.

90. *Aisha* was the favorite wife of Mohammed. She was the daughter of Abu Bekr, his best friend, and he married her while she was still very young.

91. *Boraq* was the supernatural horse upon whose back Mohammed visited heaven and returned (according to the *Hanifs*). All this was accomplished between the time a water glass was toppled over, and its contents spilled. He returned in time to catch the glass.

92. The lote tree, on the right side of the throne of Allah, figures often in the various suras of the *Koran,* and in the *Hanifs.*

93. *Abulquasim* was a given name of Mohammed.

94. *Djinns* were supernatural beings with unlimited power used chiefly for the good of man. Also called *geniis.*

95. *Hobal* was the idol worshiped by the Hashimites (Mohammed's tribe) at Mecca.

96. The *Kaaba* was the enclosure at Mecca that contained a large stone that fell from the heavens (a meteor) and about which the

pilgrims crawled on their knees seven times. It had to be rebuilt in Mohammed's day, and they brought timbers for this purpose from Jeddah, not far away.

97. The *ahl es suffa*, "people of the bench," were a group of hungry Bedouins who had been given charity by Mohammed, being allowed to drink the milk of the camels of the tithe. However, in typical Arab fashion, they killed the driver and made off with the camels. In punishment, this was the sentence passed by Mohammed and carried out.

98. One day Mohammed accidentally came upon *Zainab*, the beautiful wife of his adopted son, *Zaid ben Haritha*. She was without her veil, and partially naked. Zaid knew the nature of the Prophet. Thus, when his wife told him of the incident, he divorced her in order that Mohammed could have her. Mohammed, as usual, tried to justify his action by having a "revelation" and writing a sura of the *Koran*, but many called the marriage incestuous. Read: *Koran*, Sura XXXIII, 37, 49, 50, 51. Aisha once said to him, ironically, "I do not deny that God makes haste to satisfy your desires."

99. *Banyu Qayla*, people of Yathrib (Medina).

100. This was the opinion of Sharastani. In Wawat, *Mabahij al Fikr.*, I, 2, it is written: "The Arabean tribes were originally star-worshippers, 'Sabeans.' The people of Sheba worshipped the sun, the tribes of Asad and Kaninah, the moon, etc." This later degenerated into idolatry. According to Mohsan Fani, *Dabistan*, pp. 30–31, Abraham forbade all idols not of planetary form, and himself paid reverence to the black stone of the Kaaba, a symbol of Saturn.

101. *Nadhr ben el Harith* was one of the most radical persecutors of the Islamites during their early period in Mecca. When Mohammed would tell biblical stories, he would spoil the effect by reciting Persian legends, which he declared to be more beautiful. Following the battle of Badhr, at Es Safra, Mohammed had Ali remove his head with a sword.

102. *Razzias* were religious raids on other and neighboring tribes.

Worshipers of Mammon

103. The *uinal* was the Mayan month, a period of twenty *kins* or days. Thus, the journey required 187 days. The landing, which occurred on the seventh day of the tenth month, took place on August 6th, the tenth month of the Mayan calendar extending from July 31st to August 20th.

104. The *Sapota* was a fruit tree native to the area of Mayapan.

105. *The five nameless days* were the last five days of the year. Each year was composed of 18 months of 20 days each, and the remaining five days belonged to no month. They were called "the nameless days" and were usually spent in celebration.

106. The *codices* were the ancient Mayan books, of which only four are known to remain. They were painted on good quality paper made from the fibres of the *Agave Americana.*

107. The *Quetzal-bird,* sacred to the Mayans, belongs to the family of *Trogon resplendens.* It has a long tail and golden green feathers.

108. *Pom-incense,* which the Mexicans call Copal, was made from the pom tree, belonging to the family of *Pretium heptaphyllum.*

109. The *Moan-bird* was the deity of death, and was a species of owl.

110. For the blindness of *Zotz,* the bat, cf. *Popal Vuh,* IV. Trans. by A. Villacorta and F. Rodas, *Manuscrito de Chichicastenango,* Guatemala, 1928.

111. The *Tzental* legend of *Votan* says that he was born of the race of *Chan,* the Serpent. He appeared from across the sea, and when he reached the *Laguna de Terminos,* he named the country "The Land of Birds and Game" because of the flourishing wild-life. From the coast, he and his followers went up the *Usumacinta* Valley, and finally founded their capital at *Palenque,* the older name for which was probably *Nachan,* or "House of Snakes." Cf. Brasseur de Bourbourg, Abbé Etienne Charles, *Histoire des Nations Civilisées du Mexique et de l'Amérique-centrale, durant les Siècles anterieurs à Christophe Colomb.,* Paris, 1857–1859, Vol. I, 1, ii, pp. 68–72.

The cities of Mayapan, to the south, had long been in ruins and their builders forgotten by the time of the Spanish conquest. According to Spinden's reckoning, in the light of the *Books of Chilam Balam,* the floruit of southern Mayan culture lay in the ninth Maya cycle (160 A.D. to 554 A.D.) and included the cities of Copan, Palenque, Piedras Negras, Yaxchilan, Seibal, Tikal, and Naranjo. Morely places the end of the Great Period at about 600 A.D.

Schellhas says, in discussing the civilization of Central America: "All these facts point to a region south of the Yucatan peninsula as the true center of Central American Civilization. . . . There lie the roots of that ancient culture." P. Schellhas, *Vergleichende Studien auf dem Felde der Maya-Alterthümer, Internationales Archiv für Ethnographic,* Berlin, 1890, V, 5.

112. *Valum Chivim*—in the Tzental legend, the land to which Votan traveled.

113. *The Sowers of Flowers* and *the Men of the curved Mountain,*

were both sub-tribes belonging to the large family of Nahuatlans, the *Xochimilchos* and *Colhuas* respectively. For an account of the floating gardens, the celebrated chinampas built by the Aztecs on the surface of Lake Tezcoco, see Lucien Biart, *The Aztecs*, Chap. XIV, trans. by Garner, 1887.

114. *Mammon* (LL. *mammona*, from the Gr. *mammonas*, Aramaic: *mamona*, "riches") In the Bible, riches—hence, the God of Cupidity and Wealth.
115. Any European or American city of modern times, specifically, in this case, New York City.

Last Song of Solomon
116. "And unto Solomon did we subject the wind, which traveled in the morning a month's journey, and a month's journey in the evening, and we made a fountain of molten brass to flow for him." *Koran*, Sura XXXIV, 11. Also: "And in knowledge, Solomon was David's heir. And he said: 'Oh men, we have been endued with everything, having been taught the speech of birds and of beasts.'" *Koran*, Sura XXVII, 16.
117. Sheba was a kingdom extending from the shores of east Africa, to the narrow straits of Bab el-Mandeb, and the capital was near Sana. This journey, which was about 1400 miles, must have required at least three months.
      The Queen of Sheba, who traveled to meet Solomon, was called *Bilquis* in the *Koran*, and *Makeda* in the *Kebra Nagast*.
118. *Judah*, Judeah, the Kingdom of Israel.
119. *Ur* was a famous city of ancient Chaldea.
120. Cf. Bible, I Kings X: 10.
121. *Ophir* was a biblical land of the period, the location of which has not been determined. It was possibly somewhere in Arabia.
122. And there came to Solomon a bird which said: "with sure tidings have I come to thee from Sheba; I found a woman reigning over them, gifted with everything, and she had a splendid throne." *Koran*, Sura XXVII, 22–23, trans. by Rodwell. This bird was said to be the Hoopoe bird.
123. This description of Solomon is in accordance with Josephus, *Antiquities*, VIII, 7, 3.
124. *Etham* was a favorite pleasure garden built by Solomon, and described by Josephus. It lay two schoeni from Jerusalem—60 stadia, or about 7½ Roman miles.
125. *Ziv*, or *Zif*, second month of the Jewish calendar, and usually the beginning of the dry season. Cf. I Kings VI; 1, 37.
126. *Hebron*, ancient Kirjath-Arba, a town in south Palestine.

127. The *halil, timbrel,* and *nebel* were musical instruments of the period.

128. *Tahash* skins—the skins of some animal of the region, variety unknown.

129. According to the *Kebra Nagast,* Solomon wanted to make Makeda, the Queen of Sheba, his wife—but she refused, even though he offered to divorce all his other wives in her behalf. This rebuke hurt his pride, and that night he entertained her with a full ten-course meal of highly salted food, then saw that all the water and wines were removed from the palace except that in the carafe by his own bedside. That night, the queen, having become parched with thirst, and wandering in search of something to drink, remembered that which Solomon had reserved by the side of his bed. Solomon was awake and waiting. The result was inevitable. The son she later bore him, back in Sheba, she called *Bayna Lekhem,* "Son of the Wise Man." For the full story, read the *Kebra Nagast,* manuscript of 1320 A.D., trans. from the Abyssinian by Sir E. A. Wallis Budge.

130. Cf. I Kings VII: 1, 3; X: 18-20.

131. "It was said to her: 'Enter the Palace:' and when she saw it, she thought it a lake of water, and bared her legs. He said: 'It is a palace paved with glass.'" *Koran,* Sura XXVII, 24. Trans. by Rodwell. The *Kebra Nagast* has an interesting note on this incident. It says that, when the queen bared her legs, Solomon saw that they were covered with long black hair. But Abyssinian legend says that it was only a small patch on one heel.

132. Solomon was constantly plagued by the problem of evil, and why the evil prospered, if we are to judge by *Ecclesiastes.* Cf. Ecclesiastes II: 16; III: 19, 22.

133. Cf. I Kings II: 29-34.

134. Cf. I Kings XI: 1-3.

135. *Siloam* was a pool near Jerusalem, Cf. The Bible, John XIX: 7-11.

136. *En-gedi,* Heb., "Fountain of the Kid."

137. *Adar*—last month of the Jewish year.

138. *Tarshish.* Cf. II Chronicles IX: 21. Solomon's ships visited Tarshish.

139. *Nahash,* Heb. "serpent."

140. *Tyre* was a city of Phoenicia.

141. *Tipsah* and *Gaza* were boundary cities of Israel in Solomon's time.

142. *Carmel* was a range of hills 8 miles long, Cf. I Kings XVII: 20.

143. *Moriah* was the hill on which Solomon built his temple.

144. *Sharon* was a very fertile plain.

145. *Kidron* was a small stream. Also *Cedron.*

146. *Asher*—area unknown, possibly that once occupied by Assyria.
147. *Bulbul*, the nightingale.
148. *Molech*. Cf. I Kings XI: 7. The Ammonite god to whom living sacrifices were made. They were burned alive—largely children.
149. "And when we decreed the death of Solomon, nothing shewed them that he was dead but a worm of the earth, Shameer, that gnawed the staff that supported his corpse. And when it fell, the Djinn perceived that had they known the things unseen, they had not continued in this shameful affliction." *Koran*, Sura XXXIV, 13. Rodwell's translation. The *Talmud* also mentions the worm, Shameer, whose services were enlisted by Solomon in cutting the stones of his temple. Cf. *Talmud, Mishna, Pirke Aboth*, V; *Midrash Jalkut* on I Kings VI: 7.